Legendary Queen of England

By Michael W. Simmons

Table of Contents

Introduction

Cranmer: "Let me speak, sir,

For heaven now bids me; and the words I utter

Let none think flattery, for they'll find 'em truth.

This royal infant — heaven still move about her

—

Though in her cradle, yet now promises

Upon this land a thousand thousand blessings,

Which time shall bring to ripeness: she shall be -

But few now living can behold that goodness —

A pattern to all princes living with her,

And all that shall succeed: Saba was never

More covetous of wisdom and fair virtue

Than this pure soul shall be: all princely graces,

That mould up such a mighty piece as this is,

With all the virtues that attend the good,

Shall still be doubled on her: truth shall nurse her,

Holy and heavenly thoughts still counsel her:

She shall be lov'd and fear'd; her own shall bless her:

In her days every man shall eat in safety,

Under his own vine, what he plants; and sing

The merry songs of peace to all his neighbours:

God shall be truly known; and those about her

From her shall read the perfect ways of honour.

And by those claim their greatness, not by blood.

Nor shall this peace sleep within her: but as when

The bird of wonder dies, the maiden phoenix,

Her ashes new-create another heir,

As great in admiration as herself; "

"She shall be, to the happiness of England,

An aged princess; many days shall see her,

And yet no day without a deed to crown it.

Would I had known no more! but she must die,
—

She must, the saints must have her, — yet a
virgin;

A most unspotted lily shall she pass

To the ground, and all the world shall mourn
her.

King Henry. O lord archbishop,

Thou hast made me now a man! never before

This happy child did I get anything;

This oracle of comfort has so pleas'd me.

That when I am in heaven I shall desire

To see what this child does, and praise my
Maker."

The lines above are spoken as a prophecy upon the birth of the Princess Elizabeth towards the end of Shakespeare's *Henry VIII,* which tells the story of the courtship and marriage of the future queen's parents, King Henry VIII and Lady Anne Boleyn. The play was written after Elizabeth's death, and this passage stands as a testimonial to the deep love that her subjects felt for her throughout her life and reign.

When Elizabeth Tudor became Queen of England on November 17, 1559, her country was but a minor power on the European stage. The royal coffers were empty and England was under threat of invasion from Spain, France, and Scotland. Hundreds of people had died at the stake for heresy during the reign of Mary I, and the land was still divided, Protestant against Catholic.

Elizabeth was only 25 years old at the time of her accession, and her life had not been an easy one. She was born to a royal father who had no use for daughters. Her mother was executed on charges of adultery, treason, incest, and witchcraft when she was only three years old. As an infant, Elizabeth was the heir to the English throne—then, while still a young child, she was declared a bastard and removed from the line of succession, a demotion she was deeply sensible of even as a three-year-old. She passed her teenage years in relative obscurity, watched at every moment, manipulated by powerful men who wished to use her to further their own ambition. To protect herself, the young Elizabeth learned to be silent and watchful, studying how the greatest men in the land wielded their power, and thereby learning how to govern. Behind a modest, demure façade lay a keen and brilliant mind, stuffed with knowledge of history and theology and modern and ancient languages. The teenage Elizabeth knew there was a strong likelihood that she would one day reclaim her royal birthright, and when that day arrived, she meant to be ready.

After the birth of Elizabeth's brother, Edward, Henry VIII restored Elizabeth to the line of succession, making her an heiress of the kingdom once again. But this did not lessen the uncertainty and danger in which she lived. After the death of Edward VI, England greeted its first queen regnant—that is, a queen who rules in her own right—in the form of Elizabeth's older sister, Mary I. Now that Elizabeth was "the second person in the realm", she became the focus of even more dire plots, as Protestants conspired to depose the queen and put Elizabeth in her place. Whatever affection her sister had borne for her soon turned to fear and suspicion. Elizabeth was imprisoned in the Tower of London for three months during her sister's reign, and all the while she believed that Mary might at any moment order her to be beheaded for treason, like her mother. So certain was Elizabeth that her life was shortly to end that, when Mary died, and Elizabeth succeeded to the throne, she became convinced that God had intervened miraculously on her behalf and preserved her for some great purpose.

When Elizabeth I was crowned queen of England, she was only the second female monarch in its history. Her sister Mary had been the first, and she had ruled only three years; unhappy and unpopular, her marriage to the king of Spain had outraged her subjects. A woman, it was believed, could not possibly have the mental acuity or emotional strength to rule independently; her most significant act of governance would be to choose a good husband, who would rule in her name, by her authority. But Elizabeth did not marry. Until she was fifty years old, her advisors and Parliament alike harassed her on the subject of marriage; but although she entertained the suits of the most eligible royal bachelors of Europe, she refused them all. "I will have one mistress, and no master," she declared to her courtiers, and she proved it. By entertaining proposals of marriage from England's most powerful rivals, she maintained the balance of power in Europe in England's favor when the nation was still so weak that it might otherwise have been overrun by invaders. Her refusal to choose a husband from among her many suitors was considered, by her advisors and even some historians, to be evidence of feminine vanity, but this interpretation ignores the evident fact that, as a strategic approach to foreign relations, it was a brilliant success.

Not every royal son or daughter who inherited a throne took personal responsibility for ruling the nation; some preferred to leave it all to their advisors and councilors. As a woman, Elizabeth was expected to place most of the responsibility of government in the hands of her Privy Council. Early in her reign, her own Secretary of State,

William Cecil, once chided a foreign ambassador for allowing her to read an important state document, saying that it was too much for a woman's mind. He soon learned better, however. Elizabeth was involved at every level of government, presiding over matters great and small. She cared passionately for her people. She saw herself as having been placed by God in the role of a mother over them, and she believed that winning her subjects' love was the key to keeping her throne secure.

The prophecy written by Shakespeare was fiction, but there was another prophecy made regarding Elizabeth—or at least, a prophecy which Elizabeth seemed to fulfill. According to English folklore, Merlin once prophesied that a "Royal Virgin" would rule England, be victorious in war against the king of Spain, and found a great empire. Elizabeth was not especially interested in empire building—she never went to war with her neighbors in Europe for the sake of expanding her borders. She believed that her chief duty as monarch was to keep England at peace, so that her subjects could lead safe, stable lives in a secure realm. But during her reign, England's navy became the mightiest in the world, and her great sea captains, such as Sir Walter Raleigh, explored and founded colonies in the New World—which led, over the next four hundred years, to the founding of the vast British Empire, which would stretch across the globe.

Today, Elizabeth I remains England's most famous, most popular monarch, regarded by historians as perhaps the greatest ruler ever to sit on her country's throne. There is little to be said about her that has not been said before, but students of history continue to be fascinated by her strength, her intelligence, her originality, and her versatility. Within her own lifetime she came to be regarded as something more than regal, something almost divine—a vision of the sacred feminine whereby the cult of the Virgin Queen replaced the Catholic veneration of the Virgin Mary in newly Protestant England. As one of her principle biographers remarked, "No oblivion shall ever bury the glory of her name; for her happy and renowned memory still liveth and shall for ever live in the minds of men."

Chapter One: Princess in Peril

"Although I am not a lioness, I am a lion's cub, and bear many of his qualities."

Elizabeth I

Family and birth

On September 7, 1533, a daughter was born to Anne Boleyn, second wife of King Henry VIII of England, under a double cloud of disapproval. To her father, news of the birth of a princess came as a crushing disappointment, because he had wanted and expected a son. To many persons in England and Europe, the royal infant was no better than a bastard, the product of her father's illegal second marriage, unsanctioned by the Church. In the eyes of Henry VIII, a female heir could only destabilize the kingdom after his death; there had never been a queen in England's history, and women were considered constitutionally unfit to wield the power of the state. In the eyes of Catholics, even a son produced by Henry's union to Anne Boleyn would have been suspect. Such was the inauspicious start in life given to Elizabeth Tudor, who would become one of the most important monarchs in the history of her country, and one of the most famous queens in the history of the world.

Elizabeth's father was the son of a great hero of the English battlefield, Henry VII, a Plantagenet who founded the Tudor dynasty after defeating Richard III, last of the Yorks, at the Battle of Bosworth in 1485. Henry's oldest child, and the heir to his throne for many years, was his son Arthur; but Arthur Tudor died at the age of fifteen, the victim of a virulent disease known as the "sweating sickness", which killed large numbers of people in England in the late fifteenth and sixteenth centuries. At the time of his death, Arthur was married to Katherine of

Aragon, also fifteen years old. Katherine was the youngest child of King Ferdinand and Queen Isabella of Spain (best known to students of American history as the monarchs who commissioned Christopher Columbus's voyage to the New World.) When Arthur, Prince of Wales, died, his younger brother Henry was ten years old. He had been given a good education, but he had not been brought up to rule, and this lack of preparation for the throne was evident throughout his tumultuous reign.

It was the wish of Henry VII that his surviving son marry his brother's widow, so as to permanently cement the alliance between himself and Ferdinand and Isabella. Henry was opposed to marrying Katherine at first, but after his father's death he changed his mind. At the age of seventeen, he succeeded to the English throne, and married Katherine in the face of theological uncertainty. It was technically against canon law for a man to marry his brother's widow, because the relationship was regarded as incestuous. Henry VII had petitioned the pope for special dispensation for the marriage, which he had gained, but there were a number of irregularities surrounding the details of the dispensation that would become highly significant later on.

The marriage of Henry VIII and Katherine of Aragon produced several stillborn children, as well as a son who lived for a few weeks, but only one of their children survived infancy: Mary Tudor, later to become Mary I. Over time, the king grew obsessed with the desire for a male heir, and when Katherine turned forty, it seemed clear to him that she would not be able to provide him with one. Henry contemplated various tactics for securing a male succession, including legitimizing his bastard son Henry Fitzroy, born to one of his mistresses. Instead, he chose to petition the pope for an annulment of his marriage to Katherine, so that he could marry a younger woman capable of having children.

Henry's justification for the annulment was somewhat baroque, even by the standards of early Renaissance politics: he claimed that his marriage to Katharine was incestuous, and therefore illegal, and that the pope had no theological authority to grant the dispensation that had made the marriage possible years before. The king considered his lack of living male heirs to be proof of the marriage's theologically illicit nature, as Scripture warned that incestuous marriages would be punished with barrenness. The fact that he had a living daughter by Katharine did not signify in his eyes; only male children counted.

Henry's need to be rid of his wife led to consequences that shook the balance of power in Europe. Katherine's nephew was the Holy

Roman Emperor, who put pressure on the pope to deny the annulment. As a result, Henry decreed that England would separate from the Roman Catholic church, and that he would be the spiritual and temporal authority at the head of the new Church of England. Now the leader of his own religion, Henry could annul or otherwise dispense with as many wives as suited him.

Katherine of Aragon was stripped of her queenly status and banished from the court in 1533, reduced to the title of princess dowager, to which she was entitled as Arthur Tudor's widow. Henry married Anne Boleyn within days of the annulment, and their daughter Elizabeth was born nine months later. She would be their only surviving child. When Anne proved, like Katharine, unable to carry a male child to term, the king began to suspect her of immoral behavior. Anne Boleyn was extraordinarily cultured and well-educated for a woman of her times; politically informed, with ideas and

opinions about religion and government, she
made enemies in Henry's court who conspired
against her when the king's affection for her
began to cool. Ultimately, the clever, witty Anne
Boleyn was condemned, along with her brother
and four other men, on vague charges alluding to
incest, treason, witchcraft, and a conspiracy to
kill the king. The evidence against Boleyn and
her supposed co-conspirators was unconvincing,
but they were nonetheless executed in 1536, a
mere three years after Boleyn was crowned
queen consort.

Princess Elizabeth had been separated from her
mother when she was three months old, and
given her own household at Hatfield, in
Hertfordshire, where she was attended by nurses
and tutors. Anne Boleyn, though a fond and
doting mother, was only able to visit her there
occasionally. Elizabeth was only a toddler when
her mother was beheaded, but she was
precocious enough to take notice of the overnight

change in her status; when her attendants began to address her as "my lady Elizabeth" instead of "my lady Princess", she asked what had occasioned the change. Once the royal heir, she was now only a royal bastard, like half-sister, Lady Mary.

Not much is known of Elizabeth's feelings about her mother's death, or about her uncertain position in the world as a young child. The one thing that is known of her as a child was that she was considered to be uncommonly intelligent. In the early sixteenth century, it was fashionable for the daughters of noble households to be given the same rigorous education as boys, and Elizabeth excelled in her lessons. She spoke French, Italian, Spanish, Welsh, and Latin and could read Greek fluently. She was also proficient in the social graces that noblewomen were expected to attain, such as drawing and sewing. Her tutors considered her to be the intellectual equal of the brightest young men of the day, and though her father saw little of her during her childhood, he encouraged her education.

As evidence of the young Elizabeth's extraordinary intellectual abilities, below is a partial transcript of a letter which she wrote, at the age of eleven, to Katharine Parr, her father's sixth wife:

"TO OUR MOST NOBLE AND virtuous queen KATHERINE, Elizabeth her humble daughter wisheth perpetual felicity and everlasting joy.

NOT ONLY knowing the affectuous will and fervent zeal, the which your highness hath towards all godly learning, as also my duty towards you (most gracious and sovereign princess) but knowing also that pusillanimity1 and idleness2 are most repugnant unto a reasonable creature and that (as the philosopher sayeth) even as an instrument of iron or of other metal waxeth soon rusty unless it be continually occupied. Even so shall the wit of a man, or woman, wax dull and unapt to do or understand anything perfectly, unless it be always occupied upon some manner of study, which things considered hath moved so small a portion as God hath lent me to prove what I could do.

"And therefore have I (as for essay beginning, following the right notable saying of the proverb aforesaid) translated this little book out of French rhyme into English prose, joining the sentences together as well as the capacity of my simple wit and small learning could extend themselves. The which book is entitled, or named, The Mirror or Glass, of the Sinful Soul, wherein is contained how she3 (beholding and contemplating what she is) doth perceive how, of herself, and of her own strength, she can do nothing that good is, or prevaileth for her salvation—unless it be through the grace of God, whose mother, daughter, sister, and wife, by the scriptures she proveth herself to be.

"Trusting also that through his incomprehensible love, grace and mercy she (being called from sin to repentance) doth faithfully hope to be saved. And although I know that, as for my part, which I have wrought in it (as well spiritual as manual) there is nothing done as it should be, nor else worthy to come in Your Grace's hands, but rather all unperfect and uncorrect: yet do I trust also that albeit it is like a work which is but new begun and shapen, that the style of your excellent wit and godly learning in the reading of it (if so it vouchsafe Your Highness to do) shall rub out, polish, and mend (or else cause to mend) the words (or rather the order of my writing) the which I know in many places to be rude, and nothing done as it should be. But I hope, that after to have been in Your

Grace's hands there shall be nothing in it worthy of reprehension and that in the meanwhile no other (but Your Highness only) shall read it or see it, lest my faults be known of many. Then shall they be better excused (as my confidence is in Your Grace's accustomed benevolence) that if I should bestow a whole year in writing, or inventing ways for to excuse them.

"Praying God Almighty, the maker and creator of all things, to guarantee unto Your Highness the same New Year's Day, a lucky and a prosperous year with prosperous issue and continuance of many years in good health and continual joy and all to His honour, praise, and glory.

Henry's multiple marriages had a profound effect upon Elizabeth during her adolescence. She was nine years old when Henry's fifth wife, Katherine Howard, was arrested and executed for adultery. This event must have caused Elizabeth to reflect painfully upon her own mother's fate; supposedly, she told a friend around this time that she would never marry if she could help it. It isn't difficult to imagine that a young girl growing up in Elizabeth's circumstances would begin to conceive of marriage as a dangerous and uncertain business for a woman. And Elizabeth was in great personal danger from various political intrigues centering around her during her own youth. Though Henry had finally got his male heir from his marriage to his third wife, Jane Seymour, his son Edward was sickly, and it was uncertain whether he would live long enough to marry and produce an heir of his own.

After Edward's birth, Henry had devised a new plan for the royal succession, raising his daughters Mary and Elizabeth to the status of royal heiresses once again. If Edward died without a child of his own, Mary would inherit the throne, with Elizabeth as heiress presumptive. Mary, older than Elizabeth by seventeen years, was intensely loyal to the memory of her disgraced mother, and remained a staunch Catholic even in the face of Henry's new Reformed church. She was well loved by the English people, and, as a grown woman, was less susceptible to the manipulation of ambitious courtiers than Elizabeth, who was only fourteen when Henry VIII died in 1547.

Elizabeth, on the other hand, had been educated in the Reformed, or Protestant faith, and was a subject of intense political interest to Henry's court, which was predominantly Protestant. Edward upheld the Protestant faith, but there was considerable anxiety that he might die without an heir of his own body, and that the throne would pass to the Catholic Mary, who would purge the court of Protestants. It would be preferable, in the eyes of many, to bypass Mary and place Elizabeth on the throne, but there was no legal means of doing so.

Teenage years

After her father's death and the succession of Edward VI, Elizabeth went to live with the last of her step-mothers, Henry's widow, Katharine Parr, along with her royal cousin, Lady Jane Grey. Shortly afterwards, Katharine Parr married Thomas Seymour, whose sister, Jane Seymour, had been Edward's mother, and whose brother, Duke Humphrey, was the young king's Lord Protector. Thomas Seymour would present the teenaged Elizabeth with her first troubling introduction to personal and political intrigue.

Katharine Parr's marriage to Seymour began in scandal. Henry VIII had not yet been dead for a full year, and as his widow, Katharine was expected to live decently in retirement for the rest of her life. Furthermore, as a member of the royal family, she was not permitted to marry at all without permission of the king, young though he was. Permission and blessing for the marriage was bestowed belatedly, as a token of Edward's affection for the queen who had been most like a mother to him, but the scandal did not end there. Thomas Seymour had devised an elaborate plot whereby he would manipulate the two royal girls under his protection into marriages that would secure his power as a shadow king.

Seymour intended to arrange the marriage of Lady Jane Grey to Edward VI, her cousin, and then to marry Elizabeth himself and rule via his influence over the younger members of his family. But his attempts to groom Elizabeth for this marriage backfired. He was given to showing up in Elizabeth's private chambers before she was dressed, prompting her to rise earlier so that she would be attired and gone before he appeared. On one occasion, he cut her black mourning dress to ribbons at swordpoint, declaring that black did not suit her. When Elizabeth's governess, Kat Ashley, discovered Seymour embracing Elizabeth, she reported it to Katharine, and Elizabeth and Jane were removed from Seymour's household. Soon afterwards, Katharine Parr died as a result of complications from childbirth, and Thomas Seymour was executed for treason after he was caught in an attempt on his brother's life.

Seymour's inappropriate behavior towards Elizabeth played a large role in condemning him, and it nearly destroyed Elizabeth as well. Predatory and manipulative though Seymour had been, Elizabeth, as the king's sister, was liable to arrest and execution if she was deemed to have been a participant in immoral behavior, despite her youth. She was interrogated fiercely—the first of several such terrifying inquisitions she would face before she gained the throne—but she steadfastly denied any wrongdoing. Eventually, her name was cleared, and she returned to her own home, where she would live quietly, devoting her hours to study, for more than a decade.

It would not be surprising if her experience also fostered Elizabeth's later antipathy towards marriage; she had learned a valuable lesson about the dangers of ambitious husbands, and about the lengths that manipulative courtiers would go to in order to secure power. A woman who married surrendered her autonomy to her husband; Elizabeth had experienced enough of powerlessness during her formative years as a political pawn to have acquired a distaste for it.

Succession of Mary I

Edward VI died on July 6, 1553, after a prolonged and agonizing battle with tuberculosis. He was only sixteen, and not yet married. Thomas Seymour's brother had been ousted as Lord Protector and replaced by John Dudley, the Earl of Northumberland. Edward had inherited his father's anxieties about passing the throne to a male successor, but he was equally determined that the throne should remain in the hands of a Protestant monarch. Legally, he could not disinherit his sister Mary in favor of Elizabeth; but Dudley advised him that he could disinherit both Mary and Elizabeth on the grounds that they were illegitimate.

Next in line for the throne after Henry VIII's children were the children of his sister Mary, whose oldest daughter, Francis Brandon, was the mother of Jane Grey. Dudley, who had recently arranged the marriage of Jane Grey to his son Guildford, persuaded Edward to name Francis Brandon as his heir shortly before his death.

Brandon, having planned this move along with
Dudley, immediately relinquished her claim to
the throne in favor of her daughter. Jane Grey,
sixteen years old, was thus proclaimed queen,
against her own protests; reportedly, she fainted
when asked to sit upon the throne. Her reign
only lasted for nine days before she was deposed
and imprisoned by supporters of Mary Tudor,
who rode into London with her sister Elizabeth
at her side, and was crowned on October 1, 1553.

Wyatt's rebellion

Mary I had not long sat on the throne before her
reign became unstable, and she began to grow
deeply suspicious of Elizabeth as a consequence.
Mary's intention was to marry quickly, and to
choose a Catholic husband; this limited her
choices to foreigners, as every Englishman of
suitable rank was Protestant. When she
announced her intention to marry Philip I of

Spain, public outcry was vehement, and overturned her popular support. Those who were not appalled by the prospect of a Catholic marriage were appalled by a foreign one. It was assumed that a female monarch would give way to her husband in all things, and that Philip would become the de facto ruler of England through Mary. This provided new fuel for Protestant conspirators, who began to organize a second rebellion under Sir Thomas Wyatt and Henry Grey, Duke of Suffolk, whose daughter Jane was still a prisoner in the Tower.

Elizabeth had refrained from any involvement in Northumberland's plot to make Jane Grey queen, and she did not wish to be involved in Wyatt's plot either; but as Mary's heir, and a suspected Protestant, she was a natural, if unwilling target for conspiracy. When Wyatt's plot was discovered by the court ambassador of the Holy Roman Emperor, over ninety conspirators were arrested and executed. Wyatt, under torture, admitted that the goal had been to place Elizabeth on the throne and pressure her to marry an English noble. When Mary received word of this, she had Elizabeth imprisoned in the Tower of London and subjected to intense, relentless interrogation for over three months.

Elizabeth had been raised in the Reformed faith as a girl, but for years she had lived so quietly away from court that no official profession of faith be could ascribed to her. Since Mary had become queen and restored Catholicism as the official religion of England, Elizabeth had attended mass and performed all the outward duties of a faithful Catholic, but Mary still suspected her of Protestant leanings. Elizabeth was imprisoned in the Tower of London for three months, during which time she was in a state of constant terror that she was soon to be executed. Thomas Wyatt declared Elizabeth innocent of any role in his plot when he was on the scaffold, however, and Mary eventually released her from the Tower, though she remained under house arrest at Woodstock, a nearby manor. While at Woodstock, she wrote the following poem:

O FORTUNE! how thy restless wavering State

Hath fraught with Cares my troubled Wit!

Witness this present Prison whither Fate

Hath borne me, and the Joys I quit.

Thou causedest the Guilty to be loosed

From Bands, wherewith are Innocents inclosed;

Causing the Guiltless to be strait reserved,

And freeing those that Death had well deserved:

But by her Envy can be nothing wrought,

So God send to my Foes all they have thought.

ELIZABETH, PRISONER.

Elizabeth wrote to Mary shortly after she was imprisoned in the Tower, protesting her innocence and pleading for an opportunity to speak with her face to face.

"Let conscience move your Highness to pardon this my boldness, which innocency procures me to do, together with hope of your natural kindness, which I trust will not see me cast away without desert, which what it is I would desire no more of God but that you truly knew, but which thing I think and believe you shall never by report know, unless by yourself you hear. I have heard of many in my time cast away for want of coming to the presence of their Prince; and in late days I heard my Lord of Somerset say that if his brother had been suffered to speak with him he had never suffered; but persuasions were made to him so great that he was brought in belief that he could not live safely if the Admiral lived, and that made him give consent to his death.

"Though these persons are not to be compared to your Majesty, yet I pray to God the like evil persuasions persuade not one sister against the other, and all for that they have heard false report, and the truth not known. Therefore, once again, kneeling with humbleness of heart, because I am not suffered to bow the knees of my body, I humbly crave to speak with your Highness, which I would not be so bold as to desire if I knew not myself most clear, as I know myself most true. And as for the traitor Wyatt, he might peradventure write me a letter, but on my faith I never received any from him. And as for the copy of the letter sent to the French King, I pray God confound me eternally if ever I sent him word, message, token, or letter, by any means, and to this truth I will stand in till my death."

Whatever her suspicions about Elizabeth's religious beliefs, Mary did not dare execute her own sister without a confession to prove her guilt: the spilling of royal blood was considered taboo, especially that of a relation so near the throne. Jane Grey was not so lucky; as a result of her father's involvement in the Wyatt plot, she was executed, along with her husband, on February 12, 1554. Elizabeth considered her escape from death to be nothing short of miraculous, proof that God had listened to her prayers, and for the rest of her life she maintained the belief that God had intervened directly to raise her "from prison to the palace."

The Death of Mary I

Mary's eventual reconciliation with Elizabeth came about through the intercession of her husband, Philip of Spain. Mary had believed herself to be pregnant early in her marriage, but as the years passed and it became evident that she would not have a child of her own, she accepted the necessity of naming Elizabeth as the heir to her throne. Philip's motives in prompting this reconciliation were not entirely a matter of Christian charity; Mary's next heir after Elizabeth was Mary, Queen of Scots, who was closely allied through marriage with the French. A Protestant English queen was preferable, in the eyes of Spain, to a Catholic queen with French advisors. Furthermore, with Elizabeth as queen, Philip stood a chance of retaining his influence over English affairs; she would be expected to marry quickly, and Philip intended to offer himself to his sister in law as a prospective husband.

Mary had two false pregnancies during her marriage, marked by physical symptoms such as swelling of the abdomen. Shortly after the second of these episodes, on November 17, 1558, she became ill and died; historians have speculated that what were mistaken for signs of pregnancy were in fact symptoms of uterine cancer or ovarian cysts. Word of Mary's death was carried that same day to Elizabeth at her home at Hatfield by Sir Nicholas Throckmorton, while in Whitehall her accession was proclaimed by Parliament.

According to popular legend, Throckmorton and his men found Elizabeth seated beneath a tree when they arrived, and when they told her that she was Queen, she quoted a line from the Psalms in Latin: "This is the Lord's doing, and it is marvelous in our eyes." Shortly afterwards, she gave the first speech of her reign:

"My lords, the law of nature moveth me to sorrow for my sister; the burden that is fallen upon me maketh me amazed; and yet, considering I am God's creature, ordained to obey His appointment, I will thereto yield, desiring from the bottom of my heart that I may have assistance of His grace to be the minister of His heavenly will in this office now committed to me. And as I am but one body naturally considered, though by His permission a body politic to govern, so I shall desire you all, my lords (chiefly you of the nobility, everyone in his degree and power), to be assistant to me, that I with my ruling and you with your service may make a good account to almighty God and leave some comfort to our posterity in earth. I mean to direct all my actions by good advice and counsel.

"And therefore, considering that divers of you be of the ancient nobility, having your beginnings and estates of my progenitors, kings of this realm, and thereby ought in honour to have the more natural care for maintaining of my estate and this commonwealth; some others have been of long experience in governance and enabled by my father of noble memory, my brother, and my late sister to bear office; the rest of you being upon special trust lately called to her service only and trust, for your service considered and rewarded; my meaning is to require of you all nothing more but faithful hearts in such service as from time to time shall be in your powers towards the preservation of me and this commonwealth. And for council and advice I shall accept you of my nobility, and such others of you the rest as in consultation I shall think meet and shortly appoint, to the which also, with their advice, I will join to their aid, and for ease of their burden, others meet for my service. And they which I shall not appoint, let them not think the same for any disability in them, but for that I do consider a multitude doth make rather discord and confusion than good counsel. And of my goodwill you shall not doubt, using yourselves as appertaineth to good and loving subjects."

Chapter Two: The Young Queen

"O Almighty and Everlasting God, I give Thee most hearty thanks that Thou hast been so merciful unto me to spare me to behold this joyful day. Thou hast dealt as wonderfully and as mercifully with me as Thou didst with Daniel, whom Thou delivered out of the den from the cruelty of the raging lions. Even so was I overwhelmed, and only by Thee delivered."

Prayer of Elizabeth I before her coronation

Queen Elizabeth's court

The coronation of Elizabeth I of England took place on January 15, 1559. Her royal entry into the city of London was the first opportunity most of her subjects had to gain an impression of her. As a princess in uncertain circumstances, she had lived so modestly and retiringly, and was so little seen at court after the death of her father, that she was neither liked nor disliked, only wondered about. But she had a few trusted friends who had advised her during her years of obscurity and retirement, and she took care to keep them close during the early days of her reign, when she was establishing her court and household. William Cecil, a wealthy Cambridge-educated lawyer some thirteen years older than Elizabeth, had counseled her when she was a girl, and he would be her chief advisor for many years. He was a commoner, a son of the gentry, and thus looked down upon by many members of the royal court, but his political wisdom, and the depth of trust that existed between himself and Elizabeth, made them effective partners in the management of a kingdom that had become nearly bankrupt during Mary's reign, owing to the frequent loans she made to her husband Philip for Spain's expeditions to the New World.

Another friend who enjoyed Elizabeth's trust and favor when she first came to the throne was

Robert Dudley, whom she had known since she was a young child. It was to Dudley that Elizabeth had once remarked, as an eleven-year-old, that she never wanted to be married. When Elizabeth became queen, she invested Dudley as her Master of Horse, a position which placed him in charge of her personal transportation needs, beginning with her journey from Hatfield to London after her accession. Elizabeth's partiality for Dudley raised immediate suspicions at court. Dudley's father John, the Duke of Northumberland, had orchestrated the plot to place Jane Grey on the throne in Mary Tudor's place, and he, along with his son Guildford, had been executed for treason four years prior. Robert Dudley had been imprisoned during the investigation into his family's crimes, and though he had been cleared of wrongdoing, the name of Dudley was still suspect in the eyes of many. Dudley had been married since 1550, but his was the first of many names that Elizabeth would be connected with romantically during her reign. As her Master of Horse, he had the perfect excuse to spend hours alone with the queen during her daily rides in the country. He was also responsible for introducing her to Dr. John Dee, a scientist and supposed magician, who advised Elizabeth for many years.

Elizabeth's style as a ruler was calculated to overcome the doubts of those who believed that women were incapable of being as decisive and tough-minded as the ruler of a kingdom was required to be. At the same time, being surrounded by men, she used all the advantages available to her as an attractive young woman, flirting, crying, or having hysterics as necessary to bend her nobles to her will. She had spent her entire life studying the habits of kings and queens and scheming courtiers, and she surprised observers by stepping neatly into the role of ruler of the realm with a polished, regal air, and a carefully considered philosophy towards statecraft. She wished to be a fair minded and dignified ruler—an ambition that, perhaps, owed something to the negative example of her father. When she appointed William Cecil as her Secretary of State, she made a short speech in which she declared her wish that he would not seek to flatter her, but to give her honest counsel:

"I give you this charge that you shall be of my Privy Council and content to take pains for me and my realm. This judgement I have of you, that you will not be corrupted with any manner of gifts, and that you will be faithful to the state; and that, without respect of my private will, you will give me that counsel which you think best; and if you shall know anything necessary to be declared to me of secrecy, you shall show it to myself only' and assure yourself I will not fail to keep taciturnity therein."

Another of Elizabeth's closest confidantes was Kat Ashley, a gentlewoman twenty years older than her who had once been her governess, and was responsible for her excellent education. After Elizabeth was queen, she installed Ashley as Mistress of the Robes and First Lady of the Bedchamber, which meant that she was responsible for the royal wardrobe, and for supervising the young women who served as her maids of honor. Elizabeth had a contentious relationship with the women in her life; she was more comfortable in the company of men, and tended to perceive other women as rivals and conspirators. Her relationship with Ashley was therefore all the more important to her, as she was one of the few women she trusted implicitly.

Threats to Elizabeth's throne

Though Elizabeth remarked often and publicly that she did not mean to marry, no one, at least at the beginning of her reign, took her seriously. In England and abroad, it was assumed that this female monarch, only twenty-five years old at the time of her accession, *would* marry, and soon; the only question was to whom. Elizabeth's marrying was considered more than just politically expedient; marriage was thought to be the natural desire of all women, as well as necessary to their physical, mental, spiritual, and emotional well being. In Elizabeth's case, especially, it was thought that she would be eager to secure a husband who could relieve her of some of the enormous burden she carried, as the ruler of her country. Furthermore, there were considerable threats to the English throne and to Elizabeth's personal safety, against which marriage was considered the only safe remedy.

Many Catholics still considered Henry VIII's marriage to Anne Boleyn an illegal union, since divorce was not permitted by the Catholic faith. The fact that Elizabeth herself was Protestant made her an even more detestable choice of monarch in Catholic eyes. At the time of her accession, her closest royal relatives and potential heirs were her cousins: Lady Katherine Grey, sister of the condemned and executed Lady Jane, and Mary Stuart, Queen of Scots, wife of the Dauphin of France.

Had Henry VIII not passed the Act of Succession before his death, securing Mary and Elizabeth's places in line for the throne despite their illegitimate status, the English throne would have passed to Mary Stuart after Edward's death. Just as Protestant conspirators during the reign of Mary I had attempted to replace Mary with her cousin Jane, who was descended from Henry VIII's youngest sister, Catholic conspirators during Elizabeth's early reign wished to depose her in favor of Mary Stuart, who was descended from Henry VIII's oldest sister. There were even rumors that the pope was orchestrating an assassination plot against Elizabeth with the intention of raising Mary Stuart to the throne in her place.

Even before Elizabeth was in a position to take political action against these threats, she was moved, seemingly by instinct, to secure her throne in the most effective way possible—namely, by teaching the people of England to love her. During her first royal procession to London, she took the time to greet the commoners personally, accepting flowers and curtseys from children, listening to speeches of welcome, dispensing charity to the poor, joking and smiling with men and women alike. The Spanish ambassador, observing her interactions with the people, was stunned by the degree to which she was willing to give of herself personally to her subjects. He considered her to be overly familiar with the common people, to the point of forsaking the dignity of a queen.

But Elizabeth knew how important it was to secure the support of her subjects. Her sister Mary had not been a popular queen; having begun her reign by overcoming the Duke of Northampton's plot to replace her with Jane Grey, she was endlessly paranoid of Protestant conspiracies, and furthermore saw it as her religious duty to purge heresy from her country. This led to her ordering the persecution, arrest, torture, and execution of many Protestants—which is the reason she is still remembered today as Bloody Mary. Elizabeth, by contrast, was something of a mystery to her people when she first came to the throne, but the immensely positive first impression she made set the tone for the rest of her reign, which was characterized by comparative religious tolerance and a lack of cruelty that set her apart from most European monarchs of the late medieval and early modern period. Elizabeth's fond relationship with her subjects would lead to her being remembered as "Good Queen Bess"—as different a legacy from that of her sister as could be imagined.

When it came time for Elizabeth's coronation, on January 15, 1558, the question of religion became pressing. Elizabeth had been an outwardly practicing Catholic under Mary's reign, but her private sympathies for the Protestant faith were already suspected. The bishops of England were almost all Catholic, and they considered their duty to their faith a more pressing obligation than obedience to a new and heretical queen. During the queen's first Christmas celebrations, a few weeks before her coronation in January, she had instructed the Bishop of Carlisle, who was officiating during mass, to omit the portions of the traditional ceremony that were most offensive to Protestants. He had refused to obey this command, and celebrated the mass in the traditional way, which caused Elizabeth and her retinue to walk out of the service in protest. Likewise, during Elizabeth's coronation, the bishop refused to alter the mass to her specifications, so Elizabeth retreated to the gallery while mass was conducted.

But even this thread of discord did not mar the gorgeous spectacle of Elizabeth's coronation. She had discovered during her first royal procession that by making herself visible to the commoners and holding lavish celebrations, she could secure their affections. Her coronation was therefore specifically designed to usher in a period of celebration and thanksgiving in England, to lift the people above the suffering of their day to day lives.

Marriage

When Elizabeth had been queen only a few months, she was visited by a delegation from the House of Commons, presenting her with a formal request that she marry quickly. Elizabeth was somewhat taken aback by the boldness of the request. As the queen, her body was considered state property, to the point that foreign ambassadors routinely pried into the state of her laundry and bedsheets, seeking assurances that she menstruated normally and was fertile. Over the course of her reign, she would grow more accustomed to living her life entirely in the open, but this was her first experience of having to answer to politicians for such personal choices. She took a few days to consider the Parliamentary request in full, before issuing a detailed and thoughtful reply, quoted below:

"As I have good cause, so do I give you all my hearty thanks for the good zeal and loving care you seem to have, as well towards me as to the whole state of your country. Your petition I perceive consisteth of three parts and my answer to the same shall depend of two.

"And to the first part I may say unto you that from my years of understanding since I first had consideration of myself to be born a servitor of almighty God, I happily chose this kind of life in which I yet live, which I assure you for my own part hath hitherto best contented myself and I trust hath been most acceptable to God. From the which, if either ambition of high estate offered to me in marriage by the pleasure and appointment of my prince whereof I have some records in this presence (as you our Lord Treasurer well know); or if the eschewing of the danger of my enemies or the avoiding of the peril of death, whose messenger or rather continual watchman, the prince's indignation, was not a little time daily before my eyes (by whose means although I know or justly may suspect, yet I will not now utter, or if the whole cause were in my sister herself, I will not now burden her therewith, because I will not charge the dead); if any of these, I say, could have drawn or dissuaded me from this kind of life, I had not now remained in this estate wherein you see me. But so constant have I always continued in this determination, although my youth and words may seem to some hardly to agree together, yet is it most true that at this day I stand free from any other meaning that either I have had in times past or have at this present; with which trade of life I am so thoroughly acquainted that I trust God, who hath hitherto therein preserved and led me by the hand, will not now of his goodness suffer me to go alone.

"For the other part, the manner of your petition I do well like of and take in good part, because that it is simple and containeth no limitation of place or person. If it had been otherwise, I must needs have misliked it very much and thought it in you a very great presumption, being unfitting and altogether unmeet for you to require them that may command or those to appoint whose parts are to desire, or such to bind and limit whose duties are to obey, or to take upon you to draw my love to your likings or frame my will to your fantasies; for a guerdon constrained and a gift freely given can never agree together. Nevertheless if any of you be in suspect, that whensoever it may please God to incline my heart to another kind of life, you may well assure yourselves my meaning is not to do or determine anything wherewith the realm may or shall have just cause to be discontented. And therefore put that clean out of your heads.

"For I assure you— what credit my assurances may have with you I cannot tell, but what credit it shall deserve to have the sequel shall declare — I will never in that matter conclude anything that shall be prejudicial to the realm, for the weal, good and safety whereof I will never shun to spend my life. And whomsoever my chance shall be to light upon, I trust he shall be as careful for the realm and you — I will not say as myself, because I cannot so certainly determine of any other; but at the least ways, by my goodwill and desire he shall be such as shall be as careful for the preservation of the realm and you as myself. And albeit it might please almighty God to continue me still in this mind to live out of the state of marriage, yet it is not to be feared but He will so work in my heart and in your wisdom as good provision by his help may be made in convenient time, whereby the realm shall not remain destitute of an heir. That may be a fit governor, and peradventure more beneficial to the realm than such offspring as may come of me. For although I be never so careful of your well doings and mind ever so to be, yet may my issue grow out of kind and become perhaps ungracious. And in the end this shall be for me sufficient, that a marble stone shall declare that a Queen, having reigned such a time, lived and died a virgin."

This statement of policy—for that is what it amounted to—surprised Elizabeth's court immensely. In it, she claims that she has always preferred the life of a single, unmarried woman, and that she believes that God made her that way—that, while the majority of the women may have been divinely fashioned for marriage and motherhood, she was fashioned by God to be happy and content as an unmarried woman. This was a clever argument on her part, because it addressed the problem of her sex in a way that was difficult to answer.

England was unused to queens; Mary Tudor had been the first to reign in her own right, and what popularity she enjoyed at the beginning of her rule she quickly lost by marrying the Spanish king and persecuting Protestants. As a woman, it had been necessary for her to marry; but as a queen, responsible for the welfare of her country, she could not give way completely to her husband's wishes, as wives in the 16th century were expected to do. Mary had done her best to please Philip by allowing him to virtually bankrupt the royal treasury, but their marriage had never been a happy one, and England had been weakened by the alliance. There was considerable fear that if Elizabeth married a foreign ruler, the same thing would happen; but if she did not marry and produce an heir quickly, she was at risk of being deposed.

By sheer chance, the line of succession for the English throne was made up of an endless procession of women—but some of those women were married, and some of them already had sons, making them a potentially more attractive proposition for the monarch than Elizabeth. Parliament's suggestion was that she ought to marry an Englishman, who would then rule as de facto king in her name—but Elizabeth said she was unwilling to marry anyone who was not royal. By suggesting to Parliament that she was fashioned by God to remain single, she was challenging their notions of what constituted proper behavior for women—but she was also reinforcing the idea, originated by her father, that the kings and queens of England ruled by the will of God, and that they were specially made by Him to be fit for their office. Elizabeth was a woman, but she was also queen; by suggesting to her Parliamentary deputation that, in God's eyes, the latter trumped the former, she was laying the foundations for her own legend: that of the Virgin Queen, her most enduring moniker.

Inasmuch as it is possible to judge from comments she made that were recorded and preserved, Elizabeth seems to have been set in her heart against marriage from a very young age, for reasons that are not difficult to understand, considering the fate of her mother and her father's other wives. But just as her councilors and courtiers refused to believe that she was serious in her antipathy to marriage, Elizabeth herself fed the contradiction, encouraging foreign princes to court her and press her with marriage proposals. Elizabeth's biographer, Alison Weir, points out that, by staying single, yet allowing others to hope that she would marry, she exploited a considerable advantage in international politics. England was weak when Elizabeth came to the throne, but as long as the most powerful men in Europe were permitted to hope that she might marry one of them, they would not do anything to risk Elizabeth's good will and England's friendship.

None of the great political thinkers of her era seemed to understand that this was Elizabeth's intention; rather, they assumed that she was a victim of her own maidenly modesty, and that when she permitted foreign princes to court her, only to reject them in the end, she was gratifying her feminine vanity. Even her most trusted advisor, William Cecil, was baffled by her seeming inability to make up her mind whom to marry. Unfortunately, it would not have occurred to him that a woman, even a queen, could play such a game indefinitely without it ending in some great disaster for the nation. But it was a game Elizabeth played for the next twenty-five years, until she was no longer considered marriageable.

Religion

When it came to matters of religion, Elizabeth was considered unusually tolerant, especially compared to her own father and sister, and to inquisitorial monarchs such as Philip of Spain. She was educated in the reformed school, which emphasized intellectual development for both boys and girls, sobriety of dress, and a rejection of the "superstitions" of Roman Catholicism, such as belief in transubstantiation, or the doctrine that the wine and bread of the Eucharist were transformed into the actual blood and flesh of Christ during the mass. But Elizabeth enjoyed the rites of the Catholic mass, and permitted churches to display crucifixes (which were considered no better than idols by hardline Protestants). She would neither declare herself a faithful Catholic nor condemn Catholics categorically on exclusively religious grounds; she supported Protestant doctrinal reforms, but had no patience with puritanism.

Purists of both the Protestant and Catholic faiths were exasperated by her, but throughout her reign Elizabeth maintained the stance that religion was a matter for the conscience of the individual, not the interference of the state. Considering the degree to which religious conflict had wracked the English state for the past twenty-five years—in other words, for Elizabeth's entire lifetime—this policy relieved the people of a considerable strain. Unlike her sister Mary, who saw herself as responsible for the souls of her subjects, Elizabeth was more concerned that her realm be at peace, both internally and abroad, than that her subjects be faithful to any one set of beliefs. She would not tolerate any attempt to foment discontent and division, even by Protestants. Religious radicalism of any kind was a danger to the peace of the state, and it was treated as such.

In her private life, Elizabeth was a keen student of theological literature and read the Bible daily, spending hours alone in prayer. But she was not fond of long sermons—especially when the person delivering the sermon was using the pulpit as a platform to make pointed comments about her policies or personal habits. If a preacher bored her, she would openly cease to pay attention to him, and if he offended her, or annoyed her, she would shout at him from her seat in her private balcony until he changed topics. It was said of her after her death that, "Queen Elizabeth had rather speak to God herself, than hear another speaking of God."

Apart from the marriage question, which would not be resolved until Elizabeth was in her fifties, the major issue of her early reign was the unresolved condition of the state religion. Henry VIII had severed England's ties with the Roman Catholic church under the Act of Supremacy in 1534; it was repealed by Mary I in 1554, almost as soon as she came to the throne. Elizabeth was expected to reinstate the Supremacy Act, making the English church sovereign again, but there was one problem: Henry VIII might name himself Head of the Church without contradicting scripture, but women were expressly forbidden from holding authority in the church. The solution was a simple change of name: Elizabeth was to be referred to as "Supreme Governor" of the church. In exchange, Parliament passed the Act of Uniformity in 1559, enforcing Elizabeth's strong wish that all English churches conduct their sermons from the Book of Common Prayer that first came into use during the reign of her brother Edward VI. Elizabeth's feelings about the necessity of a common prayer book are expressed in her famous 1559 speech on religion:

"Our realm and subjects have been long wanderers, walking astray whilst they were under the tuition of Romish Pastors, who advised them to own a Wolf for their head (in lieu of a careful Shepherd) whose inventions, heresies, and schisms be so numerous, that the flock of Christ have fed on poisonous shrubs for want of wholesome pastures. And whereas, you list us and our subjects in the teeth, that the Romish Church first planted the Catholic faith within our realms, the records and chronicles of our realms testify to the contrary, and your own Romish idolatry maketh you liars; witness the ancient monument of Gildas, unto which both foreign and domestic have gone in pilgrimage, there to offer. This author testifieth Joseph of Arimathea to be the first preacher of the word of God within our realms. Long after that period when Austin came from Rome, this our realm had Bishops and Priests therein, as is well known to the wise and learned of our realm, by woeful experience, how your Church entered therein by blood, they being martyrs for Christ, and put to death because they denied Rome's usurped authority.

"As for our Father being drawn away from the Supremacy of Rome by schismatical and heretical counsels and advisers, who, we pray advised him more or flattered him than you, good Mr. Father, when you were Bishop of Rochester? And then, you Mr. Bonner, when you were Archdeacon? And you Mr. Turberville? Nay, further… who was more an adviser to our Father than your great Stephen Gardiner, when he lived? Was it not you and such like advisers that… stirred up our sister against us and other of her subjects? Whereas you would frighten us by telling how Emperors… have owned the Bishop of Rome's authority. It was contrary in the beginning, for our Saviour Christ paid His tribute unto Cæsar, as the chief superior; which shows your Romish supremacy is usurped…. We give you, therefore, warning, that for the future, we hear no more of this kind, lest you provoke us to execute those penalties enacted for the punishing of our resisters, which out of our clemency we have foreborne."

Royal Courtships

The questions of both religion and marriage came to a head over the matter of the marriage proposal of Philip of Spain. As the husband of her deceased sister, Elizabeth and Philip were barred from marrying each other, on the same grounds whereby Henry VIII claimed his marriage to Katherine of Aragon was illicit. Philip was prepared to apply for a papal dispensation to allow the marriage, but Henry VIII had asserted that the pope had no authority to grant a dispensation that contradicted the law of scripture, and Elizabeth, who was disinclined to marry Philip for many reasons, claimed the excuse that she could not dishonor her father's memory by contradicting his judgment.

Philip was as personally disinclined to marry Elizabeth as she was to marry him. He had only married her sister out of what he saw as his religious duty, a duty that was even more pressing in Elizabeth's case, since, under her rule, England threatened to fall away into heresy. His assumption, and that of his ambassador, was that she would be deeply flattered by a proposal from the most powerful ruler in Europe. But Elizabeth rejected him, while expressing the hope that the alliance between England and Spain might be just as strong and mutually beneficial without a marriage treaty to formalize the relationship. Philip, slightly offended by her refusal, but mostly relieved, agreed that the friendship between the two nations should remain strong, but he had not given up all hopes of a marital alliance between Elizabeth and his family: the two sons of the Holy Roman Emperor were also potential suitors to Elizabeth, and no sooner had Philip's suit ended than the Austrian ambassador began to press theirs. Philip's belief was that if Elizabeth could be induced to marry a Catholic prince, her own religious irregularities, and those of her realm, would soon be corrected. In this, he seemed to be overlooking the fact that it was at least partly because she was not willing to alter her religious beliefs to suit a husband that she had refused his proposal.

Alison Weir summarizes Philip's investment in the ongoing question of Elizabeth's marriage thusly:

"On 11 April [of 1559] he [Philip] sent a memorandum to de Feria, listing the advantages of such a match, and instructing the ambassador to press them home to the Queen as a matter of urgency. He was to say that, since neither archduke had a principality of his own to govern, either would be free to come and reside permanently in England. Both were eminently fitted to help her bear the burden of government, as well as being well-connected and backed by the full might of the Habsburg Empire. Thus allied, her prestige would be enhanced, both in the eyes of Europe and of her subjects, and few would dare rise against her. The price of all this would of course be Elizabeth's conversion to the Catholic faith and the surrender of her independence."

Ultimately, Elizabeth was to reject the suit of the Habsburg princes on the grounds that she would never marry a man whom she had not laid eyes on personally. She invited the younger archduke, Charles, to visit England before she answered his proposal, but she must have known when she issued the invitation that he would never accept—when marriages were arranged between royalty in the 16th century, their portraits and family names were expected to make their case for them, and for a prince to be rejected after he had taken the trouble to make a long journey would be more humiliating than royal dignity could withstand. Elizabeth rejected other suitors on these same grounds, including Prince Erik of Sweden—though he would actually attempt to meet her challenge, and travel to see her in person, only to be rebuffed twice when his ships encountered fierce storms. Elizabeth, on hearing of this, remarked that the storms were God's way of protecting her against an unwanted marriage.

Lord Robert Dudley

There were several potential English candidates for Elizabeth's hand in marriage, including the Earl of Arundel and Sir William Pickering. Arundel was unattractive and boorish, but he was immensely wealthy and descended of very ancient English noble stock. Pickering was not noble, but Elizabeth liked him and favored him with personal audiences more often than most of her courtiers. There was only one man, however, whom Elizabeth is thought to have held any personal affection for, and that is Lord Robert Dudley, son of the condemned Duke of Northumberland, who had been her friend since she was eight years old. It is scarcely surprising that Elizabeth should have deep feelings for the one man who had shown her personal loyalty since long before she was queen, or even expected to become queen, but there was another reason she could feel herself free to love him: he was married, and thus no one could pressure her to marry him.

Elizabeth enjoyed playing the game of courtly love, a stylized, almost ritualistic form of chivalry, in which a knight of the court dedicated his feats of gallantry to a high-born unavailable woman, such as a queen; flirtation was exchanged openly, but the relationship was never sexually consummated. Elizabeth made no secret of her preference for Dudley, but though it was rumored that his wife was ill and that Elizabeth was merely waiting for her to die before marrying Dudley herself, there is no evidence to suggest that she had any such intention. Nor is there any evidence that she and Dudley were having a sexual affair, though this was a popular rumor at court.

As queen, Elizabeth was scarcely ever completely alone. Her maids of honor slept in her room, and her attendants kept her in their line of sight at all times, even if they sometimes retreated out of earshot. The very fact that she flirted so openly with Dudley probably indicates that they were not sexually involved. With the examples of all her father's wives to remind her what could happen to queens who were suspected of illicit sexual conduct, if she *had* been sexually involved with Dudley, she probably would not have treated him as a favorite in open court.

Though Dudley was undoubtedly devoted to Elizabeth, her affection for him placed him in a delicate position. He was already unpopular at court; his father, grandfather, and elder brother had all been executed for treason, and yet the queen had made him her Master of Horse, an undeserved honor in the eyes of other high born courtiers whose families had never been implicated in treasonous plots. Once rumors began to circulate that Elizabeth might mean to marry him, he became, as Weir puts it, "one of the most hated men in England."

Any favorite of Elizabeth's soon became the target of courtiers and foreign ambassadors who wished to influence her indirectly—her ladies in waiting, even her laundress, were the subjects of bribes, threats, and other means of persuasion. The Spanish ambassador was among those who took notice of Elizabeth's fondness for Robert Dudley, and since Elizabeth was thought to take action based on advice Dudley was giving her in secret, he wrote to Philip that Dudley must be won over to Spain's interests. However, Dudley was already allied to Philip's interests, as it was only owing to Philip's direct intervention that Dudley had not been executed for treason alongside his father and brother in 1554.

Dudley was not entirely innocent of provoking his own unpopularity. He leveraged his favor with Elizabeth for his own gain, and he actively worked against the marriage suits of the Habsburgs and everyone else who came to court the queen. In one respect, Elizabeth and Dudley's desires were united: she did not want to marry anyone, and all of Dudley's good fortune depended on Elizabeth staying single. If she were to marry, even if her husband spent the majority of his time away from England, as Philip of Spain had done during his marriage to Mary I, she could not longer afford to flirt openly or have favorites amongst her male courtiers.

So divided was Elizabeth's court over Robert Dudley—some attempting to court his favor, others conspiring against him, both factions at each other's throats—that the queen's governess and closest friend, Kat Ashley, took it upon herself to remonstrate with Elizabeth, as a mother might do, warning her that she risked bloodshed and even civil war in her realm if she did not marry and cease flirting with Dudley in public. Ashley was so convinced that her former pupil had strayed into error that she declared she would have strangled Elizabeth in her crib as a child to prevent it. Elizabeth was not angered by Ashley's upbraiding her—she was, perhaps, the one person in the world who could claim the right to speak to the queen that way—but she felt wounded and misunderstood. She defended her behavior, declaring that she had given

"...no one just cause to associate her with her Equerry or any other man in the world, and she hoped that they never would truthfully be able to do so. But that in this world she had so much sorrow and tribulation and so little joy. If she showed herself gracious towards her Master of the Horse he had deserved it for his honourable nature and dealings... She was always surrounded by her ladies of the bedchamber and maids of honour, who at all times could see whether there was anything dishonourable between her and her Master of the Horse. If she had ever had the will or had found pleasure in such a dishonourable life...she did not know of anyone who could forbid her; but she trusted in God that nobody would ever live to see her so commit herself."

Ashley's suggestion that her friendship with Dudley was bringing trouble to her realm troubled Elizabeth as a mere false rumor about her character could not, but she was not yet prepared to give up her relationship with him. However, this did not prevent her from encouraging the Austrian ambassador to continue pressing the suit of Archduke Charles, the son of the Holy Roman Emperor. The sudden death of the king of France, Henry II, was exciting political turmoil on French and Scottish soil. Mary Stuart of Scotland was married to the Dauphin, Henry II's son, but he was young, weak, and sickly, and the French court was ruled, in effect, by his mother, Catherine de Medici. Furthermore, religious conflict was stirring in France between Catholics and Huguenots (Protestants).

There were fears in England that the tension would spread to Scotland, where the teachings of Protestant reformer John Calvin were gaining traction. French troops on Scottish soil presented an immediate and pressing risk to Elizabeth's borders in the form of an invasion from the north, and such a risk made the need for an alliance with the greatest power in Europe all the more pressing. Elizabeth may have been worried enough to genuinely consider marrying during this period in her reign, at least in vulnerable private moments, but more importantly, encouraging the Austrian courtship kept France in a state of uncertainty—for all anyone knew, England was about to become a Habsburg protectorate, and any nation considering taking a hostile action against her would be warier, with such an ally in the offing.

Refusal of Erik of Sweden

Eventually, the Holy Roman Emperor and the Archdukes of Austria retracted their marriage suit—Elizabeth had strung them along for as long as possible, but by early 1569, they began to realize that she had no intention of marrying Charles of Austria. Erik of Sweden—now king, upon his father's death—was rather more persistent. Sweden had more to gain from a marital alliance with England than the European powers, and Erik considered himself a better match for Elizabeth than most of his rival princes, because he was Protestant. His personal ardor for the Queen of England was such that Elizabeth felt he needed to be let down gently, and she penned the following letter to him as a final refusal of his proposal:

"A letter truly yours both in the writing and sentiment was given us on 30 December by your very dear brother, the Duke of Finland. And while we perceive there from that the zeal and love of your mind towards us is not diminished, yet in part we are grieved that we cannot gratify your Serene Highness with the same kind of affection. And that indeed does not happen because we doubt in any way of your love and honour, but, as often we have testified both in words and writing, that we have never yet conceived a feeling of that kind of affection towards anyone. We therefore beg your Serene Highness again and again that you be pleased to set a limit to your love, that it advance not beyond the laws of friendship for the present nor disregard them in the future. And we in our turn shall take care that whatever can be required for the holy preservation of friendship between Princes we will always perform towards your Serene Highness. It seems strange for your Serene Highness to write that you understand from your brother and your ambassadors that we have entirely determined not to marry an absent husband; and that we shall give you no certain reply until we shall have seen your person.

"We certainly think that if God ever direct our hearts to consideration of marriage we shall never accept or choose any absent husband how powerful and wealthy a Prince soever. But that we are not to give you an answer until we have seen your person is so far from the thing itself that we never even considered such a thing. But I have always given both to your brother, who is certainly a most excellent prince and deservedly very dear to us, and also to your ambassador likewise the same answer with scarcely any variation of the words, that we do not conceive in our heart to take a husband, but highly commend this single life, and hope that your Serene Highness will no longer spend time in waiting for us."

Though marriage proposals would follow Elizabeth for over three quarters of her reign, nothing would again equal the marital circus that flooded her court during the first two years after she came to the throne.

The Death of Amy Dudley

William Cecil, Elizabeth's closest advisor, was instrumental in arranging a settlement with the Scottish that protected England's northernmost border, but when he returned home expecting congratulation, he found the queen curiously indifferent to his success. Despondent, Cecil confided in the Spanish ambassador that he was thinking of resigning: he believed that Robert Dudley was responsible for edging him out of the queen's trust. He further believed that Elizabeth was determined to marry Dudley, and that nothing would stop her—not even the ruin of her entire country. He explained that there were rumors abroad that Dudley intended to have his wife murdered so that he would be free to marry the queen. Cecil knew that the Spanish ambassador would undoubtedly repeat all that he told him, and that the gossip would spread to every royal court in Europe, but this was a deliberate move on his part: he hoped that the public scandal and outcry would be so severe that Elizabeth would be forced to take note of it and regulate her actions accordingly.

Then, on September 8, 1560, a scandalous event of the gravest import rocked Elizabeth's court. Lady Amy Dudley, wife of Lord Robert, was found dead in the house where she was staying on a visit with friends. The circumstances of her death were considered deeply strange at the time, and are still thought to be mysterious to this day. The home in which Lady Dudley was staying was normally very full of visitors and family, but on the day of her death most of its inmates had gone into the nearby village to attend a fair. Lady Dudley had been particularly insistent that her servants should go, and when some protested that they did not think it was appropriate to attend a fair on a Sunday, she became angry and insisted they leave. Around noon, she had lunch with a friend; a few hours later, the servants returned home and found her lifeless body lying at the bottom of a short staircase.

The news of her death was delivered to Lord Robert and to Elizabeth at the same time; both were intensely shocked, and both understood that Lord Robert would be suspected of having arranged his wife's murder, unless it could be absolutely proven that he was innocent. Furthermore, any marriage between them would now be impossible—regardless of the verdict of the inquest, it would always be whispered that Lord Robert had killed his wife in order to be free to marry the queen. Lord Robert departed from court instantly, on Elizabeth's order, while investigations were made into Lady Dudley's death. The inquest soon ruled the death an accident, though Lady Amy's personal maid believed she might have committed suicide. This was not the news that Lord Robert had hoped for, however. If the inquest had ruled her death a murder, and yielded evidence leading to the arrest of the guilty party, his name would have been cleared in a far more decisive war. A verdict of accidental death left room for whispers that Lord Robert had been responsible for arranging the accident.

Though Lord Robert was popularly supposed to have wished his wife dead, and to have the best motive for arranging a fatal accident, he did not ultimately profit from her death in the slightest. The only person who did benefit by it was William Cecil, who, once Lord Robert had been banished from the court, was restored to his former place in the queen's trust. Certain historians have even gone so far as to theorize that Cecil himself might have arranged for Lady Dudley to be murdered. It was he, after all, who first mentioned to the Spanish ambassador that there were rumors that Lord Robert meant to do away with her. And it was Cecil who was most sensible of the danger to Elizabeth's throne should she marry Dudley—a marriage which was made impossible by the suspicious death of his wife. There is no evidence of Cecil's involvement, however, and there is no way of further investigating one of the greatest royal scandals of all time.

The gossip in foreign courts was such that Sir Nicholas Throckmorton, one of Elizabeth's oldest supporters and her ambassador to France, wrote to William Cecil that,

"I wish I were either dead or hence, that I might not hear the dishonourable and naughty report that are made of the Queen, and the great joy among the French princes for the success they take it they are like to have in England—not letting to speak of the Queen and some others, that which every hair on my head stareth and my ears glow to hear. One laugheth at us, another threateneth, another revileth the Queen. Some let not to say, 'What religion is this, that a subject shall kill his wife, and the prince not only bear withal but marry with him?' If these slanderous bruits be not slaked, or if they prove true, our reputation is gone forever, war follows, and utter subversion of the Queen and country."

Elizabeth, finally realizing she had no choice but to take action to quell the rumors that she intended to marry Dudley, subjected him to a rather severe public humiliation: he had been asking her for some time to make him an earl, and she went so far as to have the official papers drawn up and a ceremony of investiture begun— only to destroy the papers publicly and declare that she would not have another member of Dudley's family made a peer of the realm, after his father, brother, and grandfather had all been executed for treason. Dudley was incensed, but he remained at her side and in her favor. Meanwhile, the indignity she had subjected him to served to quell the gossip that she intended to marry him, and though the rumors that he had killed his wife would follow Dudley for the rest of his life, he remained by Elizabeth's side and in her favor for some time yet to come.

Chapter Three: The Royal Succession

"VERY DEAR SISTER,—If it were not a thing impossible that one should forget her own heart, I should fear you suspected that I had drunk of the waters of Lethe. But I assure you that besides there being no such river in England, so of this fault you are the principal cause. For if the waiting for your messenger, who, as you wrote to me, ought long since to have come hither, had not so much delayed [me], I would have visited your by my letters according to our previous custom. But when I heard that you were going on such a long pilgrimage to so great a distance from hence, I thought that would hinder you from receiving my note. On my part there was another occasion which hindered me greatly, the fear of tiring you with hearing the tragedies, with which every week my ears have been all too much wearied. Would to God they were as hidden to others as they have been concealed by me. And I assure you on my honour that right up till when the ravens croaked of them, I kept my ears sealed up like those of Ulysses. But when I saw that all my councillors and subjects thought me of sight too dim, of hearing too deaf, of spirit too improvident, I roused myself from such slumber, and deemed myself unworthy to govern a kingdom, such as I possess, if I were not also skilled in my own affairs: a Prometheus, as well as acquainted with Epimetheus.

"And when it came to my mind how it touch your kinsfolk, Mon Dieu, how I gnawed my heart! Not for them (you know it well), but for her on whose behalf I long for all the good that can be desired, having a great fear lest you should think that the old sparks would be fanned by this new fire. Notwithstanding, when I saw that necessity had no law, and that it behoves us carefully to guard our houses from spoil, when those of our neighbours are ablaze so close at hand, I have not even so much as a suspicion that you would refuse to draw away nature's veil and gaze on the naked cause of reason.

"For what hope is left for strangers when cruelty so much abounds among those of the family? I would sooner pass over in silence the murders on land than tell in writing of the burials in water, and would say nothing of men cut in pieces, if the cries of pregnant women strangled with the wails of infants at their mothers' breasts did not stir me. What rhubarb drug will purge away the choler which these tyrannies engender?"

Letter from Elizabeth I of England to Mary Stuart of Scotland, 1562

Heirs to the throne

Elizabeth's advisors were desperate for her to marry because, as a woman, she was considered unfit to rule; but also because it was desperately important that she produce an heir, and quickly. The significance of heirs is perhaps difficult for the modern student of history to grasp, but in the 16th century, transfer of power without bloodshed was a rare event. A clear, legitimate line of succession, preferably from father to son, was seen as a bulwark against factionalism and civil war. For this reason, Henry VIII named his daughters Mary and Elizabeth as his heirs after his son Edward, even though he himself had declared them illegitimate, and never reversed that ruling. Even a bastard child of the old king was a preferable successor to some lesser known cousin, especially when there were multiple cousins related to the king to an equal decree— there was always the possibility that they would fight one another over the throne.

Because the Tudors were anything but a fruitful dynasty, Elizabeth's potential heirs presumptive ran to a seemingly endless line of female cousins, all of whom she feared to one degree or another. Her fears were not entirely to do with anything personal about them; Elizabeth knew what it was to *be* a royal heiress, how it had made her the target of conspiracies and her sister's own paranoia. She did not wish to lay that burden on anyone. Moreover, the moment she selected and authorized an heir, she would be in danger from plots to imprison her and raise her successor to the throne prematurely, particularly if her successor were married. It cannot be overstated how deeply uncomfortable 16th century Englishmen were with having a queen, a woman whom they could not overrule and who had no husband to do it for them. There were undoubtedly many who would have been pleased to see another woman in her place, so long as she came equipped with a husband. Elizabeth was given to remark that having her counselors insist on her naming a successor was rather like being forced to contemplate her own death. To the Scottish ambassador, she remarked,

"Think you that I could love my winding sheet, when, as examples show, princes cannot even love their children that are to succeed them? I have good experience of myself in my sister's time, how desirous men were that I should be in place, and earnest to set me up. It is hard to bind princes by any security where hope is offered of a kingdom. If it became certainly known in the world who should succeed me, I would never think myself in sufficient security."

Katherine Grey

One of Elizabeth's more troublesome cousins was Lady Katherine Grey, the younger sister of the condemned Lady Jane Grey, some seven years Elizabeth's junior and the next in line for the English throne, according to the succession plan devised by Henry VIII. Elizabeth had a personal antipathy towards Katherine, who, though she had been raised Protestant, had converted to Catholicism after her sister and father were executed, and had in consequence been made one of Queen Mary's maids of honor. Katherine, as a Catholic, deeply interested the Spanish ambassador, who could foresee a time when England and Spain might once again be united under a common rule—if he could arrange for Katherine Grey to marry King Philip's heir, that is.

Henry VIII had passed a law making it a matter of treason if a person of royal blood, like Katherine Grey, married without the express consent of the monarch, no doubt to avoid scenarios like the one the Spanish ambassador was contemplating. But Katherine, only twenty years old, fell in love with Edward Seymour, Earl of Hertford, whose father had been Lord Protector under Edward VI. With the encouragement of Katherine's mother, and the assistance of Edward's sister, the two were secretly married—a secret they were only able to keep until Katherine discovered that she was pregnant in March of 1561. Katherine begged for Elizabeth's mercy, but Elizabeth responded by having both Katherine and Hertford imprisoned in the Tower, in separate cells. Furthermore, she had the marriage declared illegal, thus ensuring that the baby boy to whom Katherine gave birth a few months later was illegitimate, and not another potential heir to the throne. There was no longer any question of officially instating Katherine as Elizabeth's heir; if nothing else, the secret marriage had proven that Katherine was prone to acting rashly without considering consequences, which made her unfit for the throne in Elizabeth's eyes.

Mary Stuart, Queen of Scotland

Elizabeth's other dynastically significant cousin, Mary Stuart, had been Queen of Scotland almost since she was born. But for most of her life she had lived in France, in the court of Henry II, to whose son, the Dauphin Francis, she was betrothed. Scotland, in the mean time, was ruled by her mother, Marie de Guise, who was Regent. Mary and Francis were very fond of one another, growing up together as playmates before they were married in 1558, when Francis was 15 and Mary was 16. The next year, Francis came to the throne of France after Henry II died of wounds obtained in a jousting match; however, he reigned for only a few months before dying of an ear infection, leaving Mary widowed and the French court under the control of her mother in law, Catherine de Medici, acting as Regent for her ten year old son Charles. Catherine de Medici did not like Mary, and wasted no time in suggesting that, as she was sovereign of her own kingdom, perhaps she ought to return there. Mary did as she suggested, and her journey back to the British Isles brought her to the attention of Elizabeth.

Mary Stuart, or at least the idea of her, had long been a thorn in Elizabeth's side. Henry VIII had excluded the Stuarts, descendants of his sister Margaret, from the line of succession. The French, however, considered Elizabeth a bastard and a heretic, and therefore, when Mary I died shortly after Mary Stuart and Francis were married, Henry II declared his new daughter in law the rightful Queen of England, and ordered her coat of arms to display the royal arms of England, as a way of driving the point home. It is therefore scarcely surprising that Elizabeth regarded Mary as a threat to her crown.

When Mary Stuart was widowed and sent back to her own kingdom, however, relations between her and Elizabeth changed. It was necessary for the two queens to be on friendly terms with one another. Scotland had recently established its own Protestant government in their Catholic queen's absence, but it was rumored that Mary intended to restore the old faith, which might spark a religious war that would spill over the border. (In fact, faced with an overwhelming Protestant majority in Scotland, Mary chose to institute a policy of complete religious freedom, which permitted her subjects to worship according to their conscience while she practiced Catholicism in private.)

But Elizabeth could not help feeling a rivalry with her. Queens regnant were such a novelty in the 16th century that it was impossible to avoid comparisons between the two women. Mary's husband was dead, leaving her 18 years old, single, and Catholic, in addition to being Queen of Scotland and a potential heir to throne of England. She was, in short, now the most desirable royal bride in all of Europe—and Elizabeth knew there was a chance that all the foreign princes who had been desperately courting her might now turn their attention to her younger, less heretical, and (it was rumored) prettier cousin. Elizabeth's command over men was an integral aspect of the political mechanism by which she ruled. Mary Stuart threatened to upset that balance in more ways than one. Nonetheless, Elizabeth was also sensible of the fact that, as a fellow queen and a family member, she had more in common with Mary than with practically anyone else in the world. She was curious as to what Mary was like, and had a great curiosity to meet her.

After Mary's arrival in Scotland, her ambassador to England began attempting to arrange a formal state visit in York, a northern English city that served as an approximate halfway point between the homes of the two queens. Both Mary and Elizabeth were deeply eager to lay eyes on one another, and they began to exchange friendly letters. Mary hoped that Elizabeth would name her as her successor, and Elizabeth hoped to influence Mary's choice of husband, in order to prevent her from marrying a powerful Catholic prince who might threaten England's borders. The visit was arranged, but when hostilities broke out between Catholics and Huguenots in France, Elizabeth felt that her Protestant subjects might react badly if she were to play host to a Catholic monarch. She canceled the visit, to Mary's intense disappointment, and though Elizabeth promised to reschedule it, the visit never took place.

Health crisis

In late 1562, Elizabeth contracted a case of smallpox—one of the most virulent killers of its day, a disease feared as much for its ability to disfigure as for its mortality rate. For several days, her life was despaired of—her fever climbed, she gradually lost the ability to speak, and for over twenty four hours she was unconscious.

Her councilors were, understandably, panicked: the line of succession was anything but clear, and the strongest legitimate claimant to the throne, Mary Stuart, had no supporters amongst Elizabeth's most important advisors. Civil war seemed inevitable, if Elizabeth should die. During her periods of lucidity, the queen instructed that Lord Robert Dudley should be named Lord Protector of England if she should die, to safeguard the realm until a successor should be found. Her councilors, though not necessarily in agreement with the choice, assured her that it would be done as she asked— no one was willing to jeopardize her health by arguing with her.

When Elizabeth rallied and recovered from her illness, it was nearly time for the second Parliament of her reign to gather. She postponed the assembly for as long as she could—she knew, given the recent health scare, that she would be pressed, again, to marry, and quickly. But she could not delay forever, and when the delegation came from the House of Commons, she listened carefully to what the Speaker of the House had come to say to her, and responded thus:

"I have heard by you the common request of my Commons which I may well term (me thinketh) the whole realm because they give, as I have heard, in all these matters of Parliament their common consent to such as be here assembled. The weight and greatness of this matter might cause in me, being a woman and wanting both wit and memory, some fear to speak and bashfulness besides, a think appropriate to my sex... Great cause may justly move me in this so great a matter touching the benefit of this realm and the safety of you all to defer mine answer till some other time, wherein I assure you the consideration of my own safety (although I thank you for the great care that you seem to have thereof) shall be little in comparison of that great regard that I mean to have of the safety and surety of you all.

"And though God of late seemed to touch me rather like one that he chastiseth than one that he punished, and though death possessed almost every joint of me, so as I wished then that the feeble thread of life which lasted methought all too long, might by Clotho's hand have quietly been cut off; yet desired I not then life (as I have some witnesses here) so much for mine own safety as for yours. For I knew that in exchanging of this reign I should have enjoyed a better reign, where residence is perpetual. There needs no boding of my bane. I know now as well as I did before that I am mortal. I know also that I must seek to discharge myself of that great burthen that God hath laid upon me, for of them to whom much is committed, much is required. Think not that I, that in other matters have had convenient care of you all will in this matter touching the safety of myself and you all be careless. For I know that this matter toucheth me much nearer than it doth you all who, if the worst happen, can lose but your bodies. But if I take not that convenient care that it behooveth me to have therein, I hazard to lose both body and soul.

"And though I am determined in this so great and weighty a matter to defer mine answer till some other time because I will not in so deep a matter wade with so shallow a wit, yet have I thought good to use these few words as well to shew you that I am neither careless nor unmindful of your safety in this case, as I trust you likewise do not forget that by me you were delivered whilst you were hanging on the bough ready to fall into the mud, yea to be drowned in the dung; neither yet the promise which you have here made concerning your duties and due obedience, wherewith I assure you I mean to charge you, as further to let you understand that I neither mislike any of your requests herein nor the great care that you see to have of the surety and safety of your helps in this matter. Lastly because I will discharge some restless heads in whose brains the needless hammers beat with vain judgement, that I should mislike this their petition, I say that of the matter and sum thereof I like and allow very well. As to the circumstances, if any be, I mean upon further advice further to answer. And so I assure you all that though after my death you may have many stepdames, yet shall you never have any a more natural mother than I mean to be unto you all."

Both houses of Parliament were so affected by Elizabeth's extraordinary powers of oratory that they ceased to pressure her on the subject of marriage for the time being. It was felt that Elizabeth understood the danger posed to the realm, and that she would take her councilors' advice and marry soon. She had, in fact, promised no such thing, but she had purchased the breathing room she needed to attend to other matters. Over the next few years, rumors increased that she would marry Robert Dudley, who was now the Earl of Leicester. He was no longer so viciously unpopular as he had once been, and William Cecil had begun to regard him more favorably since his wife's death. The feeling of Elizabeth's councilors was that she must marry as quickly as possible, and it no longer mattered so much who she married, as long as she produced an heir.

Elizabeth had a different idea for Dudley's fate, however. By April of 1564, she had begun writing to Mary Stuart with hints that she should marry one of Elizabeth's high born English subjects; she did not mention Robert Dudley by name at first, but she pressed Dudley's suit upon the Scottish ambassador in her court. The ambassador was not impressed by the suggestion that his queen should marry a man who had been suspected of murdering his last wife, much less a man whom many in England considered too low born for their own queen. Furthermore, he found it difficult to believe that Elizabeth was serious about parting with her favorite courtier. She had only grown closer to Dudley over the years, appointing him to the Privy Council, restoring Warwick Castle to his elder brother along with the lands that had been stripped from the Dudley family when their father had been executed for treason. Dudley even occupied the suite of rooms closest to the queen's in the palace of Whitehall. Yet it seems that Elizabeth was serious about the proposed marriage, despite the fact Dudley had no desire to leave England for Scotland, which he regarded as a land of barbarians. As it happened, Mary Stuart herself found the idea of a marriage to Dudley insulting, though before long, she was embroiled in a love affair with another Englishman, one who was a distant cousin of Elizabeth's: Henry Stuart, Lord Darnley. They would marry in July of 1565, to widespread consternation.

Chapter Four: Troubles in Scotland

King Henry Stuart

Henry Stuart, Lord Darnley, was a direct descendant of Elizabeth's grandfather, Henry VII—which meant that, by marrying him, Mary Stuart had only strengthened her claim on the English throne. But otherwise, Darnley was not a politically astute match. Mary's own councilors reviled the prospect of their marriage as much as Elizabeth did. Mary was in love, however; in the words of one of her advisors, she was "so altered with affection towards Lord Darnley that she hath brought her honor into question, her estate into hazard, her country to be torn in pieces. I see also the amity between the countries [England and Scotland] like to be dissolved, and great mischiefs like to ensue."

Mary's advisors considered Darnley arrogant and possessed of poor judgment, and Mary herself would eventually come to see his true character and exclude him from her councils, making decisions independent of his advice. To his fury, she refused to name him king consort, or to invest him with any official authority; in response to his repeated insistence that she name him as her co-ruler, she gave him the title of "king", a concession very nearly insulting in its meagerness. Worse still, Mary's friendship with Elizabeth deteriorated beyond the hope of mending as a result of the marriage. Darnley was an English lord, and Mary had insulted Elizabeth by marrying one of her subjects and kinsmen without gaining, or even asking, royal permission. When Mary's half brother, the Earl of Moray, began a rebellion against her, Elizabeth gave him unofficial support in the form of a small sum of money, and he was permitted to live in exile in England when the rebellion failed, although Elizabeth could not bring herself to receive a traitor, even a traitor to a rival queen, warmly.

Darnley succeeded in alienating Mary Stuart's affections almost entirely within only a few months of their marriage. Instead, she turned to her secretary, an Italian by the name of David Rizzio, for guidance, advice, amusement and friendship. This incensed both Darnley, who suspected Mary of having an affair with Rizzio, and the Protestant lords who resented Mary's intimacy with a Catholic and a foreigner. When Mary became pregnant in 1565, Darnley became convinced that Rizzio was the father, and with the assistance of Protestant lords, conspired to murder him. In March of 1566, Darnley and a group of nobles burst in on Mary's private chambers, and, threatening the queen at gunpoint to prevent her from interfering, dragged Rizzio into the hallway and stabbed him over fifty times.

The intended result of the murder plot was complicated: Lord Darnley, thinking that the stress of witnessing the murder might force Mary to miscarry her pregnancy, hoped to be named regent or even king in her place while she recovered. Even if she survived the ordeal unscathed, his co-conspirators promised to imprison Mary and set him up in her place. Unbeknownst to Darnley, his co-conspirators were as eager to be rid of him as they were to be rid of David Rizzio, and they intended to persuade the queen that the entire plot had been Darnley's idea, hoping that she would then have Darnley executed for treason. Mary and Darnley were imprisoned together for two days after the murder, but Mary, who was less intellectual than Elizabeth but far more intelligent than her husband, managed to extract the full details of the plot from him. At her instigation, they escaped together and raised an army to march on the rebellious lords, who fled the city to avoid her. Mary lost all trust in Darnley afterwards, and would keep him at a distance from her councils for the rest of what remained of his life.

William Cecil was sent word of the plot in time to have prevented it, but chose not to interfere or to apprise Elizabeth in advance. When Mary herself wrote to Elizabeth after her escape, she was deeply shocked and distressed, and promptly informed the Spanish ambassador, who had spent years trying to persuade her to marry the Archduke Charles of Austria, that if any husband of hers had served her thus, she would have seized his dagger and stabbed him with it. Elizabeth's friendship with Mary was temporarily restored due to the solidarity Elizabeth felt with her fellow queen, whose safety and authority had been endangered in so rough a manner. They resumed writing to one another, and Mary asked Elizabeth to be godmother to her baby when it was born. Unbeknownst to either queen at the time, the infant, James, born on June 19, 1566, would become far more than

Elizabeth's godson: as James VI of Scotland and James I of England, he would become Elizabeth's heir and successor, and unite the two countries under one crown.

The birth of James Stuart provoked yet another attempt by Parliament to pressure Elizabeth into marrying, which annoyed her to the point of fury. She had been badgered to marry since the very beginning of her reign, and she was tired of it. Marriage was a personal matter, and she was the queen; it was for her to decide when and whom she would marry, and Parliament's continual insistence upon the point verged on disrespect. Elizabeth summoned a small delegation from the House of Commons to the palace, where they were not permitted to speak, only to listen as she replied, at length, and in typically brilliant and blistering fashion, to their latest recommendation:

"Was I not born in the realm? Were my parents born in any foreign country? Is not my kingdom here? Whom have I oppressed? Whom have I enriched to other's harm? What turmoil have I made in this commonwealth that I should be suspected to have no regard to the same? How have I governed since my reign? I will be tried by envy itself. I need not to use many words, for my deeds do try me.

"Well, the matter whereof they would have made their petition (as I am informed) consisteth in two points: in my marriage, and in the limitations of the succession of the crown, wherein my marriage was first placed, as for manners' sake. I did send them answer by my council, I would marry (although of mine own disposition I was not inclined thereunto) but that was not accepted nor credited, although spoken by their Prince.

"I will never break the word of a prince spoken in a public place, for my honour's sake. And therefore I say again, I will marry as soon as I can conveniently, if God take not him away with whom I mind to marry, or myself, or else some other great let happen. I can say no more except the party were present. And I hope to have children, otherwise I would never marry. A strange order of petitioners that will make a request and cannot be otherwise assured but by the prince's word, and yet will not believe it when it is spoken.

"The second point was for the limitation of the succession of the crown, wherein was nothing said for my safety, but only for themselves. A strange thing that the foot should direct the head in so weighty a cause', a cause, she pointed out, to which she had give careful consideration since it concerned her more nearly than it concerned them.

"I am sure there was not one of them that ever was a second person, as I have been and have tasted of the practices against my sister, who I would to God were alive again. [That is, none of the people pressing her to name a successor had ever been second in line to the throne, as she had been when her sister Mary was queen. Then, Elizabeth had been accused of fomenting rebellion against her sister.] . . . .

"There were occasions in me at that time, I stood in danger of my life, my sister was so incensed against me. I did differ from her in religion and I was sought for divers ways. And so shall never be my successor. . . .

"They would have twelve or fourteen limited in succession and the more the better. And those shall be of such uprightness and so divine, as in them shall be divinity itself. Kings were wont to honour philosophers, but if I had such I would honour them as angels that should have such piety in them that they would not seek where they are the second to be the first, and where the third to be the second and so forth. It is said I am no divine. Indeed I studied nothing else but divinity till I came to the crown; and then I gave myself to the study of that which was meet for government, and am not ignorant of stories wherein appeareth what hath fallen out for ambition of kingdoms--as in Spain, Naples, Portugal and at home; and what cocking hath been between the father and the son for the same. You would have a limitation of succession. Truly if reason did not subdue will in me, I would cause you to deal in it, so pleasant a thing it should be unto me. But I stay it for your benefit.

"I do not marvel, though Domini Doctores, with you my Lords, did so use themselves therein, since after my brother's death they openly preached and set forth that my sister and I were bastards. Well, I wish not the death of any man, but only this I desire, that they which have been the practisers herein may before their deaths repent the same, and show some open confession of their fault, whereby the scabbed sheep may be known from the whole. As for my own part I care not for death, for all men are mortal; and though I be a woman yet I have as good a courage answerable to my place as ever my father had. I am your anointed Queen. I will never be by violence constrained to do anything. I thank God I am indeed endowed with such qualities that if I were turned out of the realm in my petticoat I were able to live in any place in Christendom.

"Your petition is to deal in the limitation of the succession. At this present it is not convenient, nor never shall be without some peril unto you, and certain danger unto me. But as soon as there may be a convenient time and that it may be done with least peril unto you, although never without great danger unto me, I will deal therein for your safety and offer it unto you as your prince and head without requests. For it is monstrous that the feet should direct the head."

It may seem odd that Elizabeth, being queen, should find Parliament's combative attitude so offensive, but as it happened, she needed them to call a vote and pass a subsidy bill, without which she had no funds to operate her court. Having lived outside the glamor of royal courts for most of her life before she came to the throne, Elizabeth had a horror of exceeding her means, and always lived within them frugally—a rare trait for any head of state in any age—but she did require some money in order to conduct affairs of state. Her frugality gave her a certain amount of leverage over Parliament, but ultimately she could not stop them from raising the marriage question as many times as they saw fit.

The Death of Henry Stuart

Meanwhile, in Scotland, the brief rapprochement between Mary Stuart and her husband Lord Darnley after the murder of David Rizzio had long since come to an end. Darnley was still a fixture at Mary's court, but she scarcely ever saw him—though she was perpetually on tenterhooks after the birth of their son, for fear that Darnley would provoke some new scandal while the castle was full of foreign princes and their representatives, come to attend the christening of the infant James. No sooner was the christening over than Mary began looking for ways to divest herself of Darnley for good. Religious avenues were closed to her; she could not have their marriage annulled without making the infant James illegitimate, so she turned to the very same Scottish lords who had conspired with Darnley to kill David Rizzio for assistance. In return for Mary's pardon for the murder of Rizzio, they promised to manage the matter on her behalf. She insisted that "nothing must be done to stain [her] honor and conscience", but the injunction was not taken seriously.

Since the death of David Rizzio, Mary had turned for help and friendship to another man, James Hepburn, the Earl of Bothwell, who had sheltered her and Darnley after their escape from Glasgow. Though Bothwell never admitted his involvement, it was probably upon his instigation that Darnley was murdered in Edinburgh in February of 1567. Mary had left Darnley alone at a house called Kirk o' the Field late the previous evening to attending a wedding nearby. Around two o'clock the next morning, while she was still away, there was an explosion at the house, and when the villagers rushed to investigate, they found Darnley and his manservant lying upon the ground outside with their throats cut.

Mary affected to be shocked and distressed when news reached her, claiming that her husband had been the mistaken victim of an assassination plot against herself. Whether or not Mary knew of the plot to murder Darnley is a matter for historical conjecture. The assassins may not have been acting with her full knowledge and consent, but she may have been aware what her nobles had in mind when they promised to help her get rid of her husband. Or perhaps she was just as surprised as she seemed to be, and her quick recovery was a powerful act of queenly self-control. But the people of Scotland were quick to assume that Mary and Bothwell had been co-conspirators in Darnley's death, largely because it was soon evident that Bothwell stood to benefit from it in a very material way—namely, by marrying the queen. Back in England, Elizabeth received a detailed report on the royal murder from William Cecil, and she quickly wrote a short note to Mary, reproduced below:

"Madam: my ears have been so astounded and my heart so frightened to hear of the horrible and abominable murder of your former husband, our mutual cousin, that I have scarcely spirit to write; yet I cannot conceal that I grieve more for you than him. I should not do the office of a faithful cousin and friend if I did not urge you to preserve your honor, rather than look through your fingers at revenge on those who have done you that pleasure, as most people say. I exhort you, I counsel you, I beg you, to take this event so to heart that you will not fear to proceed even against your nearest. I write thus vehemently, not that I doubt, but for affection."

It is a curious note, in light of what Elizabeth may have believed about Darnley's murder. This was the same man whom Elizabeth declared that she would have stabbed, had she been in Mary's place the night of Rizzio's murder. She cannot have failed to suspect that Darnley's death was less of a mystery to his wife than she was pretending it was. Was Elizabeth's advice merely practical, encouraging her cousin to find a scapegoat for the murder in order that she might distance herself from the blame? Or did she actually find herself disturbed by the lengths to which Mary had proven herself willing to go to safeguard her crown? Elizabeth's advisors had always spoken of her seat on the throne as shaky, in need of foreign aid and male assistance to prop it up, but in comparison to Mary, she was fairly secure. Perhaps she was forced into contemplating what measures she herself might be willing to resort to, were her rule ever threatened so directly and personally as Mary's had been.

The Abduction of Mary Stuart

In any event, Mary's apparent unwillingness to punish her husband's murderers was a severe strike against her in the eyes of her people, and in the opinions of foreign nobles. But what followed was far more damning. Darnley's parents, the Earl of Lennox and Lady Lennox, attempted to bring Bothwell up on charges, but the Scottish justice system at that time was arranged on principles not dissimilar to trial by combat. When a lord such as Lennox had a complaint to make against a lord such as Bothwell, the custom was for both men to meet at an appointed place after gathering as many supporters as they were able; whoever had the largest display of men won the trial. In this case, Bothwell was able to gather a much larger number of men than the Earl of Lennox, who chose not to attend the trial at all once it became apparent that he would lose. In this way, Bothwell avoided facing any formal charges.

Two weeks after the trial, Mary's period of mourning for her husband came to an end, and whilst she was traveling back to Edinburgh after paying a visit to her infant son, she was abducted by Bothwell and his eight hundred men, who forced her to ride to Bothwell's castle at Dunbar. There, Bothwell raped the queen, knowing that she would feel that she had no choice except to marry him afterwards. Bothwell was himself married at the time, but his wife obtained a divorce from him for adultery a few months later, and the wedding took place then. There has been a great deal of historical speculation on this subject, just as with the murder of Darnley, regarding whether Mary knew what Bothwell intended to do and had consented to it in advance, but there is no evidence for this. Bothwell had a reputation for being a dangerous and ruthless man. The body and person of an unmarried queen was seen as the most valuable piece of property in the country, and a man as unscrupulous as he might dare much to obtain it.

Elizabeth, upon receiving news of the event, was stunned that Mary had agreed to be married to the man who had abducted her; it is not certain whether she knew of the rape. She wrote the following note in May or June of 1567:

"Madam, it has been always held in friendship that prosperity provideth but adversity proveth friends, wherefore we comfort you with these few words... To be plain with you, our grief has not been small threat: for how could a worse choice be made for your honour than in such haste to marry a subject who, besides other notorious lacks, public fame has charged with the murder of your late husband, besides touching yourself in some part, though, we trust in that behalf, falsely. And with what peril have you married him, that hath another lawful wife, nor any children betwixt you legitimate. Thus you see our opinion plainly, and we are heartily sorry we can conceive no better. We are earnestly bent to do everything in our power to procure the punishment of that murder against any subject you have, how dear soever you should hold him, and next thereto to be careful how your son the Prince may be preserved to the comfort of you and the realm."

Elizabeth, no doubt, could scarcely resist making a comparison between her own decision to temporarily distance herself from Lord Robert Dudley until he was cleared of all suspicion in his wife's death, and Mary's apparent intimacy with Bothwell, who was accused of murdering her husband. But Elizabeth was not in possession of all the facts. She did not know, for instance, that Mary was suicidal in the days immediately following the wedding. Bothwell was a Protestant, and he had forced her to be married in a Protestant ceremony, which, for a woman of Mary's strong Catholic beliefs, was no marriage at all; in her own eyes, she was living in sin with the man who had raped her. It was whispered that, on their wedding night, Bothwell had confessed to Mary his true role in murdering Darnley, and she was appalled. It was also whispered that Bothwell had persuaded Mary to believe that he was in love with her only until their marriage, and that immediately afterwards he returned to his ex wife for companionship. Whatever she might have felt towards Bothwell before the abduction, rape, and wedding, it was plain to all observers that he made her miserable once he was her husband.

How differently might Elizabeth have felt or acted towards Mary in the years that followed had she been giving a more complete accounting of events in Scotland that spring and summer? Based on what she did know, she found Mary's behavior disgusting and shameful—Mary was the one person in all the world to whom she could compare herself, and Elizabeth could not imagine having been so weak in the face of danger. But Elizabeth had had to steel herself to face danger continually all through her life until she came to the throne; Mary, by contrast, had lived a sheltered existence, brought up in the French court on the expectation that she would be queen and co-ruler of both France and Scotland with her husband. Elizabeth coveted her independence, but Mary wished to be married. And while Elizabeth was a canny and sophisticated political thinker, Mary, though not stupid, had not been educated to Elizabeth's level. Apart from the fact that they were queens and cousins, Mary Stuart and Elizabeth Tudor were not particularly alike at all—but because they were both queens, Elizabeth could not help judging Mary according to her own strict, self-imposed standards, and Mary suffered a great deal in the comparison.

Miserable though Mary's marriage with Bothwell was, it had at least the virtue of being short-lived: the Scottish lords liked Bothwell as little as they had liked Darnley, and wasted no time in driving him out of Scotland. In June of 1567, Mary was taken prisoner by her own lords and Bothwell was forced to flee for the sanctuary of Denmark. Mary was paraded through Edinburgh on her way to Lochleven, an island fortress that would serve as her dungeon, where she was told that she might choose either to stand trial for conspiring to murder Darnley, to abdicate her throne in favor of her son James, who was still a toddler, or to divorce Bothwell. She refused all three options: her religion forbade divorce, she dared not abdicate and allow her son to be controlled by the Scottish lords who had murdered his father, and as an anointed sovereign, she was answerable for her actions to no one except God. She could not stand trial because no one had the jurisdiction to try her. Evidence had been produced against her in the form of the "Casket Letters", an extended correspondence between herself and Bothwell that implicated Mary as an adulteress and co-conspirator in Darnley's death. These letters were almost certainly a forgery, as Mary had been taught from childhood to write her letters in cipher in case they were stolen or intercepted, but there was no way for her to prove that. It was already plain to her that the people of Scotland hated her; in Edinburgh, the crowds had shouted and thrown things at her, calling her a whore and a murderer. She had no hope of an impartial trial, even if she had been willing to participate in one.

Elizabeth, though exasperated and disappointed by Mary's behavior on a personal level, was profoundly alarmed by the idea of a queen being imprisoned by her subjects. She sent one of her nearest advisors, Sir Nicholas Throckmorton, to Scotland with a three-fold agenda: to restore Mary to the throne, to see the murderers of Lord Darnley arrested, tried, and condemned, and to look out for the safety of Mary's son James— Elizabeth wanted James brought to England to be looked after and protected, if possible. Throckmorton was fully sensible that this was the most dangerous diplomatic mission he had ever been sent on, but as it happened, he was not permitted to see the queen in Scotland before she was forced to abdicate in July. Having recently miscarried twins, losing a dangerous amount of blood in the process, it nonetheless took the threat of having her throat cut on the spot to force her to cooperate.

Even after her abdication, Mary probably would have been murdered were it not for the fact that her cousin Elizabeth was threatening to rain hellfire down on Scotland's lords for their role in their queen's humiliation. "What warrant have they in Scripture to depose their Prince?" Elizabeth demanded. "Or what law find they written in any Christian monarchy, that subjects may arrest the person of their Prince, detain them captive and proceed to judge against them? No such law is to be found in the whole civil law... We will take plain part against them to revenge their sovereign, for an example to all posterity." Elizabeth was, plainly speaking, so incensed against the Earl of Moray, Mary's half-brother and Regent for James VI, that she recalled her ambassador, refused to acknowledge the legitimacy of the boy king, and threatened war against Scotland continually until the autumn of that year.

Chapter Five: Uprisings and Rebellions

Collapse of marriage negotiations with the Habsburg dynasty

In the winter of 1567, after eight years of courtship stretching back to the very beginning of her reign, Elizabeth at last gave a definitive refusal to the proposal of marriage made to her by the Holy Roman Emperor, Ferdinand II, on behalf of his son, the Archduke Charles of Austria. He had, for the better part of a decade, been considered the most favorable match Elizabeth could make. After she had refused the proposal of Philip of Spain, her advisors had lamented the missed opportunity to make a marital alliance with the Habsburgs, the wealthiest and most powerful royal dynasty in Europe; the Archduke was seen as a final shot at such an alliance. Philip of Spain had been vocal in his wish for the marriage to take place; he believed that by marrying a Catholic prince, Elizabeth, and thus England, could be won back for the Catholic faith.

It was on religious grounds that Elizabeth made her final refusal. Though the Archduke was Catholic, he had, after much negotiation, agreed to be married in a Protestant ceremony and accompany Elizabeth to Protestant services, so long as he and his Austrian household were allowed to attend Catholic mass in private. This would be a violation of Elizabeth's own Act of Uniformity; furthermore, remembering how unpopular Philip had been in England during his marriage to Mary I, she was convinced that her subjects would hate the Archduke just as much.

In the 16th century, Spain controlled much of the Protestant Netherlands, where William of Orange was leading a religious rebellion against the Catholic forces. England and Spain had been on friendly terms while the Habsburg marriage was still under consideration, but when those negotiations came to an end, friendly relations between Spain and England were no longer assured. Elizabeth recalled her ambassador to the Spanish court; the Spanish ambassador to England was replaced with someone less personally sympathetic to the queen. And when Philip sent a garrison to thwart the Protestant forces in the Netherlands, they were stationed in Brussels, near enough to England's border to make Elizabeth wary of antagonizing Spain by assisting William of Orange. Elizabeth's response was to take measures that quietly strengthened England's navy.

The imprisonment of Mary, Queen of Scots

In May of 1568, Mary escaped from her prison at Lochleven with the assistance of her servants, and attempted to lead a force of six thousand men against the Scottish lords who had forced her abdication. They were swiftly defeated, however, and in a panic, Mary and a few attendants fled the country in disguise until they reached England, where Mary begged for Elizabeth's protection and assistance in taking back her throne. Elizabeth was much disposed to give it to her; she still could not abide the fact that a lawful queen had been deprived of her throne, and she felt that any amount of impossible odds or negative political repercussions should be dared to restore Mary to her rightful place.

Elizabeth's advisors, however, including William Cecil, were far less enthusiastic towards Mary's cause. They pointed out that, saving when she was in trouble and needed Elizabeth's assistance, Mary had never been a sound ally to Elizabeth or England. Furthermore, Cecil had been corresponding with the Scottish Regent, the Earl of Moray, since his rise to power, and considered him an able governor and a good replacement for the rule of the Queen of Scots. It was Cecil's opinion that Mary ought to be sent back to Scotland immediately. But this, Elizabeth was not willing to do, knowing that Mary would be apprehended and executed almost immediately. But keeping her in England was a prospect similarly beset with dangers, if not to Mary, then to Elizabeth herself. The Spanish garrison in Brussels, for instance, was conveniently placed to invade England and act as a revolutionary force that could depose Elizabeth and put the Catholic Mary on the throne in her stead.

Elizabeth elected to place Mary in what amounted to protective custody at Bolton Castle in Yorkshire under the supervision of Sir Francis Knollys, one of her most trusted advisors. She would not receive Mary at her own court until Mary had been publicly cleared of wrongdoing in the death of Lord Darnley, a decision which upset Mary greatly. She was somewhat mollified when Elizabeth promised to do all that she could to restore her to her throne once a proper inquiry had been made into the Darnley affair and the Earl of Moray's role in having Mary deposed, but only somewhat. Elizabeth had conditions for her assistance. Chiefly, she wanted Mary to, finally and forever, reject all claim to the throne of England, which she had hitherto refused to do. Mary was willing to cooperate if it meant that Elizabeth would assist her in taking back her throne, but she soon had reason to regret asking for Elizabeth's help. During the inquiry, the so-called Casket Letters were produced, and though Mary insisted that they were forgeries, Elizabeth, after reading them, became convinced of their authenticity. She had not allowed Mary to testify publicly before the tribunal, but she did offer Mary the opportunity to answer the accusations against her in writing, as appears in the letter which Elizabeth wrote to her in December of 1568:

"Madame, whilst your cause hath been here treated upon, we thought it not needful to write any thing thereof unto you, supposing always that your commissioners would thereof advertise as they saw cause; and since they have broken this conference, by refusing to make answer, as they say, by your commandment, and for that purpose they return to you, although we think you shall by them perceive the whole proceeding, yet we cannot but let you understand by these our letters, that as we have been very sorry of long time, for your mishaps and great troubles, so find we our sorrows now doubled in beholding such things as are produced to prove yourself the cause of all the same. And our grief herein is increased, in that we did not think at any time, to have seen or heard such matter of so great appearances and moment to charge and condemn you.

"Nevertheless, both in friendship, nature, and justice, we are moved to cover these matters, and stay our judgement, and not to gather any sense thereof to your prejudice, before we may hear of your direct answer thereunto, according as your commissioners understand our meaning to be, which at their request is delivered to them in writing. And as we trust they will advise you for your honor to agree to make answer, as we have mentioned them, so surely we cannot but as one prince and near cousin regarding another, most earnestly as we may in terms of friendship require and charge you not to forbear from answering.

"And for our part we are heartily sorry and dismayed to find such matter of your charge, so shall we be as heartily glad and well content to hear of sufficient matter for your discharge; and although we doubt not, you are well certified of the diligence and care of your ministers having your commission, yet can we, not besides and allowance generally of them, specially note to you your good choice of the bearer the Bishop of Rosse, who hath not only faithfully and wisely, but also so carefully and dutifully, for your honor and weal, behaved himself, and that both privately and publicly, as we cannot but in this sort commend him unto you as we wish you had such devoted discreet servants; for in our judgement, we think, ye have not any in loyalty and faithfulness overmatch him: and thus we are the bolder to write, considering we take it the best trial of a good servant, to be in adversity, out of which we wish you to be delivered, by the justification of your innocence. And so trusting to hear shortly from you, we make an end. Given at Hampton Court, under our signet, the 21st of December, 1568, in the eleventh year of our reign."

Mary was not willing to make a formal answer in writing to the charges laid against her because she denied that Elizabeth had any right or authority to try her. Faced with this lack of cooperation, and fairly convinced of Mary's guilt, from this point forward Elizabeth ceased all attempts to restore her cousin to the throne of Scotland. Because Mary chose to offer no defense to the charges made against her, the verdict returned was one of "not proved"—that is, neither guilty nor innocent. Elizabeth's judgment was that Mary should live, from then on, a quiet life of relative ease and comfort, under the protection and guard of such persons as Elizabeth should appoint. Elizabeth was not entirely contented with this outcome. She knew already that having Mary in England would tempt Catholics to mount a rebellion to depose her and put Mary in her place. For the time being, however, there were no good alternatives.

The Ridolfi plot

England's relationship with Spain was deteriorating by the end of the 1560's, owing partly to maritime mischief on the part of England. A sizeable sum of cash had been seized from Spanish ships foundering on the English coast, and Elizabeth had elected not to return it to Philip of Spain, which, understandably, made Philip furious. The seizure of the Spanish cargo had been done on William Cecil's authority, making him the target of a complicated plot against Elizabeth's throne.

Dukes, earls, and lords from the north of England, where Catholicism was still deeply entrenched, conceived a plan to restore Mary Stuart to the Scottish throne, restore amicable relations between Spain and England, and maintain the alliance between Scotland and England. To do this, agreed the Duke of Norfolk, the Earl of Arundel, and Robert Dudley, Earl of Leicester, they must first deprive William Cecil of his place on the Privy Council; then, a marriage would take place between the Duke of Norfolk and Mary Stuart. It came to be called the Ridolfi plot after an Italian banker, Roberto Ridolfi, who was enlisted by Norfolk to approach Philip of Spain on his behalf, asking for his support in the plot, and promising in exchange to re-establish Catholicism in England. Philip, however, was not interested, but Mary was. She responded to Norfolk's marriage proposal with delight, believing that it would help her to regain her throne.

Leicester eventually came to realize that his own queen, were she kept any longer in the dark, would regard this plot as a form of treason; though she wanted to see Mary Stuart returned to Scotland in her rightful place, she knew it was far more likely that Mary would make a bid to become queen of England, with Norfolk at her side. Norfolk was not yet deliberately plotting against Elizabeth, but he knew that he stood in danger of her retaliation if he confessed to her that he had proposed marriage to her cousin. Fear of her retribution eventually drove him to retreat into his estates in the north. A popular uprising of Catholics was being organized in the area: funded by Roberto Ridolfi, organized by the Earl of Northumberland and the Earl of Westmorland, and encouraged by the Spanish ambassador, it stood a serious chance of successfully deposing Elizabeth if Norfolk should join forces with them.

Norfolk, however, chose to obey the queen's command that he attend her at court. He wrote to the Earl of Westmorland before he left, begging him to call off the rebellion. Elizabeth was incensed against Norfolk, but Cecil assured her that there was no evidence that his intentions had been treasonous, so she imprisoned him temporarily in the Tower of London, and dealt with his matrimonial ambitions in a practical manner: lest he should be tempted to pay court to Mary Stuart again,

Cecil should find him a better, safer sort of wife. Meanwhile, Northumberland and Westmorland led their uprising, but it was quickly defeated. The goal of the uprising had been to rescue Mary Stuart and place her on the throne; but the castle where she was kept was too well guarded.

Catholic threats to the crown

Elizabeth took the uprising very much to heart, and she ordered swift, severe reprisals against the rebels. As Alison Weir puts it, "reprisals were unusually savage, and no village was to be without at least one execution, 'the bodies to remain till they fall to pieces where they hang'. By 4 February 1570, between 600 and 750 commoners had been hanged and two hundred gentry had been deprived of their estates and goods, which were distributed to loyal noblemen." It was around this time that Elizabeth finally began to seriously consider the recommendations of her councilors that Mary Stuart be put to death.   It was becoming apparent to her that for long as the Queen of Scots lived, she would be a convenient focus for any Catholic plots against Elizabeth's reign.

Elizabeth had good reason to fear an increase in Catholic plots against her: in February of 1570, Pope Pius V formally excommunicated her, and the encyclical he published, *Regnans in Excelsis,* reproduced in excerpt below, not only absolved all faithful Catholics in England from their allegiance to her, but declared that any Catholic who followed her laws would henceforth be declared a heretic.

"1. ...But the number of the ungodly has so much grown in power that there is no place left in the world which they have not tried to corrupt with their most wicked doctrines; and among others, Elizabeth, the pretended queen of

England and the servant of crime, has assisted in this, with whom as in a sanctuary the most pernicious of all have found refuge. This very woman, having seized the crown and monstrously usurped the place of supreme head of the Church in all England to gather with the chief authority and jurisdiction belonging to it, has once again reduced this same kingdom- which had already been restored to the Catholic faith and to good fruits- to a miserable ruin.

"2. Prohibiting with a strong hand the use of the true religion, which after its earlier overthrow by Henry VIII (a deserter therefrom) Mary, the lawful queen of famous memory, had with the help of this See restored, she has followed and embraced the errors of the heretics. She has removed the royal Council, composed of the nobility of England, and has filled it with obscure men, being heretics; oppressed the followers of the Catholic faith; instituted false preachers and ministers of impiety; abolished the sacrifice of the mass, prayers, fasts, choice of meats, celibacy, and Catholic ceremonies; and has ordered that books of manifestly heretical content be propounded to the whole realm and that impious rites and institutions after the rule of Calvin, entertained and observed by herself, be also observed by her subjects...

"3. We, seeing impieties and crimes multiplied one upon another the persecution of the faithful and afflictions of religion daily growing more severe under the guidance and by the activity of the said Elizabeth -and recognizing that her mind is so fixed and set that she has not only despised the pious prayers and admonitions with which Catholic princes have tried to cure and convert her but has not even permitted the nuncios sent to her in this matter by this See to cross into England, are compelled by necessity to...declare the foresaid Elizabeth to be a heretic and favourer of heretics, and her adherents in the matters aforesaid to have incurred the sentence of excommunication and to be cut off from the unity of the body of Christ.

"4. And moreover (we declare) her to be deprived of her pretended title to the aforesaid crown and of all lordship, dignity and privilege whatsoever.

"5. And also (declare) the nobles, subjects and people of the said realm and all others who have in any way sworn oaths to her, to be forever absolved from such an oath and from any duty arising from lordship. fealty and obedience; and we do, by authority of these presents, so absolve them and so deprive the same Elizabeth of her pretended title to the crown and all other the above said matters. We charge and command all and singular the nobles, subjects, peoples and others afore said that they do not dare obey her orders, mandates and laws. Those who shall act to the contrary we include in the like sentence of excommunication."

The encyclical did not have quite the effect that the Pope intended. Rather than inciting Elizabeth's Catholic subjects to rise against her, it merely made them an object of persecution by loyal and patriotic Protestants. Even the Catholic monarchs of Spain and France, who had promoted Catholic interests and plots in England in the past, condemned the bull and declared that the Pope had gone too far. Still, Elizabeth would not mimic her sister's approach to governance and use the authority of the state to prosecute Catholics. Those Catholics who committed treason were tried for treason, not for heresy. Catholics who remained faithful subjects, though technically forbidden from practicing their faith by the Act of Uniformity, suffered very little: non-attendance at Protestant churches was punished only by a very small fine, which in many cases was never collected.

This changed somewhat in 1571, when Elizabeth's spy network, under the direction of Sir Francis Walsingham, learned that Roberto Ridolfi, the Italian banker, was again corresponding with Mary Stuart. Mary had given up all hope of Elizabeth's assisting her to regain her throne, and was turning to foreign Catholic allies for help. Norfolk was again implicated; having narrowly escaped severe punishment for his previous involvement with the Scottish queen, and having sworn to Elizabeth to have nothing to do with her in future, he was once again drawn into a marriage scheme. He had better hopes of success now than previously: the Duke of Alva, commanding a large number of Spanish soldiers, would invade England, while Norfolk roused English Catholics to fight in the north. Mary would be queen, and Norfolk her king. Restrictions on English Catholics tightened in response to the intelligence; they were no longer permitted to own rosaries, crucifixes, or icons, nor could they possess copies of any papal bull, even apart from the one that excommunicated Elizabeth. Nonetheless, when the Ridolfi plot failed for good, it failed because there were not enough Catholics in England willing to rise up against their queen. Despite the fact that many Protestants regarded all Catholics as traitors in waiting, the vast majority were too loyal to Elizabeth to support Norfolk's cause. In the end, Norfolk's correspondence with Mary Stuart was discovered; he was arrested for treason, and persons close to Mary revealed the entire conspiracy.

Parliament was determined that Elizabeth should have Mary executed for her involvement in the plot, but Elizabeth could not bring herself to do it. In the final account, Mary was a fellow queen who had fled to Elizabeth's realm for protection, and Elizabeth, having granted it, felt that she could scarcely execute her now. She did, however, execute the Duke of Norfolk, after much agonizing. She had refused to sign his death warrant when it was first brought to her. Never before had any of her subjects been executed for treason during her reign, and she greatly disliked delivering capital sentences. As William Cecil remarked of her, "The Queen's Majesty hath always been a merciful lady and by mercy she hath taken more harm than justice, and yet she thinks she is more beloved in doing herself harm. God save her to His honour long among us."

Troubles with Spain

Elizabeth made repeated attempts to get Mary Stuart off her hands by secretly requesting the regency government in Scotland to make demands for her return to Edinburgh, where she would be tried for the murder of her husband. The Scots wanted nothing to do with her, however; as unpopular as she was, they would not kill their own queen if they could safely leave her in England as Elizabeth's prisoner. Mary, realizing that she could never regain her own crown, redoubled her efforts to usurp Elizabeth's after the Ridolfi plot failed. She wrote letters in code to her powerful Catholic allies in Europe, including the Pope and Philip of Spain, letters which she did not realize were being intercepted and read by Sir Francis Walsingham, whose spies were watching her every move.

Relations were tense between England and Spain in the late 1570's. Philip's Protestant subjects in the Netherlands were in rebellion against him, and a few years before, in France, over ten thousand Huguenots had been slaughtered in the Massacre of St. Bartholomew. Elizabeth wished to support the Protestant cause in Europe, and she continued to feel uneasy about the presence of a large number of Spanish soldiers in the Netherlands, near her own borders. But when the people of the Netherlands offered her their crown, she could not bring herself to accept it; just as it was unthinkable that she should have Mary Stuart killed, it was unthinkable to her to accept the rule of a country that already had a divinely anointed sovereign in Philip. Secretly, however, she supported the Protestant rebels with money and arms.

Courtship of the Duke of Anjou

Elizabeth was yet again forced to contemplate a marriage proposal, owing to the Protestant insurrections in the Low Countries. Francis, the Duke of Alençon and Anjou, brother of King Henry II of France, had Protestant sympathies. He proposed to drive the Spanish out of the Netherlands, marry Elizabeth, and rule the two Protestant countries jointly. Elizabeth was pleased to entertain his suit; regardless of her private feelings about marriage, she always enjoyed the process of courtship, both personally and for the advantages it brought to England. A marital alliance between France and England would be particularly welcome in light of the growing discord with Spain. But she had heard reports that Anjou himself was severely pockmarked and had a deformed spine; furthermore, Elizabeth was by now 45 years old, while Anjou was only 24, and she was afraid that the gap in their ages would make her seem ridiculous in the eyes of the world.

Anjou distinguished himself from the rest of her many suitors by coming to see her in person; other princes had considered it beneath their dignity to come to England without first being assured that a marriage would take place. Once she laid eyes on him in person, all Elizabeth's personal objections were swept away. They became extremely close during his stay at Elizabeth's court, exchanging presents and sitting up together late at night, much to the jealousy of Robert Dudley, who was declining in

Elizabeth's favor somewhat since his secret Lettice Knollys, one of Elizabeth's ladies of honor, which had taken place without royal permission.

When Anjou was forced to cut his visit short and return to France after a close friend was killed in a duel, Elizabeth wrote the following poem—one of the finest sonnets of the mid-16th century, proof that her talents were not limited to statecraft:

> I grieve and dare not show my discontent,
>
> I love and yet am forced to seem to hate,
>
> I do, yet dare not say I ever meant,
>
> I seem stark mute but inwardly do prate.
>
> I am and not, I freeze and yet am burned,
>
> Since from myself another self I turned.

My care is like my shadow in the sun,

Follows me flying, flies when I pursue it,

Stands and lies by me, doth what I have done.

His too familiar care doth make me rue it.

No means I find to rid him from my breast,

Till by the end of things it be supprest.

Some gentler passion slide into my mind,

For I am soft and made of melting snow;

Or be more cruel, love, and so be kind.

Let me or float or sink, be high or low.

Or let me live with some more sweet content,

Or die and so forget what love ere meant.

It is possible that, at this stage in her life, having enjoyed years of independence, Elizabeth was genuinely considering marriage. But her councilors were violently opposed to the match. Some suggested that her subjects would rebel if she were to present them with a French king so soon after the Massacre of St. Bartholomew. Others had finally come to the conclusion that the queen should never marry, for fear that she would die in childbirth if she were to become pregnant at her advanced age. Elizabeth was so angered by the publication of a pamphlet condemning the proposed marriage that she ordered the author imprisoned and his right hand cut off—a not unheard of punishment in the 16th century, but one that was uncharacteristic of Elizabeth's reign. She continued to correspond with Anjou for some time, but the knowledge that she would lose the support of her subjects ultimately prevented the marriage. She allowed the motions of the courtship to continue another two years, but this she did for strategic reasons.

Chapter Six: The Death of Mary, Queen of Scots

Mistress of Seafarers

Starting at about the midpoint of Elizabeth's reign, English sea explorers had been opening new trade routes and exploring new lands. They also, to the gratification of themselves and their queen, and the furious mortification of the Spaniards, routinely boarded and plundered Spanish merchant ships, keeping a portion of their stolen treasure for themselves and remitting a portion to Elizabeth. Sir Francis Drake was the most famous of the Elizabethan privateers. In 1580, after seizing eight hundred thousand pounds' worth of Spanish treasure, Philip of Spain began to call for Drake's head; Elizabeth, however, entertained Drake at court as an honored guest. The honor shown to Drake infuriated the Spanish ambassador, and relations between England and Spain began to deteriorate even more sharply. Angered by the fact that Elizabeth would not stop or punish English pirates who interfered with Spanish trade, Philip was beginning to plan a major naval offensive against England. Elizabeth, little caring how offended Philip would be, elevated Francis Drake to the knighthood during a feast she attended aboard his own ship.

Since Elizabeth was excommunicated, special seminaries had been established throughout Europe to train priests for "the English mission": to go into a land where Catholicism was forbidden and support those English subjects who remained faithful. However, these seminaries served a secondary purpose. The new pope, Gregory XIII, had re-issued the bull against her, and had furthermore stated that any Catholic lord of England who undertook Elizabeth's assassination "with the pious intention of doing God service" was absolved of any sin in the murder. Elizabeth's courtship with

Anjou was doubly important as a consequence—whether or not she meant to marry him, a French-English alliance was the surest security against Spanish-Catholic plots. Anti-Catholic laws in England became all the more severe—any converts to that faith were arrested as traitors, and those arrested might potentially be subject to illegal torture to make them give up the names of fellow Catholics. Philip, in consequence, saw fit to warn Elizabeth via his ambassador that she risked war if she did not cease to persecute English Catholics.

Elizabeth responded by informally betrothing herself to Anjou in an impromptu ceremony whereby she gifted him with a ring and accepted his ring in return, in full view of the entire court and several ambassadors. For a time, it seemed beyond all doubt that Elizabeth and Anjou would truly marry. However, the French king, Henry III, made it a condition of the marriage contract that Elizabeth should fund Anjou's wars in the

Netherlands, and this, Elizabeth was unwilling to do. However, Philip of Spain was sufficiently unnerved by the seeming inevitability of England's alliance with France that he made overtures to Elizabeth, offering a new alliance between them and forgiveness for England's past offenses, including piracy against Spanish ships. This concession made up slightly for the fact that Anjou refused to leave England until Elizabeth had bribed him with tens of thousands of pounds.

Sir Walter Raleigh

Apart from Sir Francis Drake, the most notable seafarer of Elizabeth's time was Walter Raleigh, who was the great-nephew of Kat Ashley, Elizabeth's childhood governess. According to legend, Raleigh first brought himself to Elizabeth's attention by throwing his jacket over a puddle to protect her slippers from the mud during a royal progress; the historical accuracy of this story cannot be verified, but such dramatic gestures were characteristic of his nature.

Raleigh recommended himself to Elizabeth by virtue of his extensive learning and truly Renaissance list of accomplishments. Like Francis Drake, he regaled her with tales of his travels and sea voyages. He was not popular at court, however; customary favorites of the queen such as Leicester were deeply jealous of him. Raleigh made enemies freely with his arrogance and argumentativeness, and though he was elected a member of Parliament, Elizabeth did not allow him to rise very high amongst her circle of advisors; for instance, he was never admitted to the Privy Council. But she granted him many other favors and honors, including, in 1584, her royal warrant to establish colonies in the New World, a portion of which is reproduced below:

"ELIZABETH by the Grace of God of England, France and Ireland Queen, defender of the faith, &c. To all people to whom these presents shall come, greeting. Know ye that of our especial grace, certain science, and mere motion, we have given and granted, and by these presents for us, our heirs and successors, we give and grant to our trusty and well-beloved servant Walter Raleigh, Esquire, and to his heirs and assigns for ever, free liberty and license from time to time, and at all times for ever hereafter, to discover, search, find out, and view such remote, heathen and barbarous lands, countries, and territories, not actually possessed of any Christian Prince, nor inhabited by Christian People, as to him, his heirs and assigns, and to every or any of them shall seem good, and the same to have, hold, occupy and enjoy to him, his heirs and assigns for ever, with all prerogatives, commodities, jurisdictions, royalties, privileges, franchises, and pre-eminences, thereto or thereabouts both by sea and land, whatsoever we by our letters patents may grant, and as we or any of our noble progenitors have heretofore granted to any person or persons, bodies politic or corporate: and the said Walter Raleigh, his heirs and assigns, and all such as from time to time, by license of us, our heirs and successors, shall go or travail thither to inhabit or remain, there to build and fortify, at the discretion of the said Walter Raleigh, his heirs and assigns, the statutes or acts of Parliament made against fugitives, or against such as shall depart, remain or continue out of our Realm of England without license, or any other statute, act, law, or any ordinance whatsoever to the contrary in anywise notwithstanding."

The warrant authorized Raleigh to take possession of any land not already belonging to another European monarch. The establishment of an English outpost in the New World offered an advantage in any potential naval conflict with

Spain. Raleigh would fall out of favor with Elizabeth in later years for marrying one of her maids of honor, Elizabeth "Bess" Throckmorton, without royal permission, but he would also play a role in the defense of the English coast off Devon during the upcoming battle of the Spanish armada.

The Babington Plot

Mary Stuart had not ceased to plot against Elizabeth in the years since the Ridolfi plot was foiled. She continued to write letters, coded and ciphered, to her friends in Europe, unaware that Sir Francis Walsingham was copying her letters and having them deciphered before they were passed along to her. Mary's co-conspirators included her Guise relations in France, the Jesuit priests who had been infiltrating England for the last several years, and the Spanish ambassador to England, acting for Philip of Spain, as well as Catholics in Ireland, Scotland, and elsewhere. In Spain, the plot was known as the Enterprise of England: it aimed to stir up a Catholic rebellion in England and simultaneously invade with a Spanish force that would arrest Elizabeth and put Mary on the throne in her place.

Elizabeth's advisors were still calling for Mary to be executed, and Elizabeth still refused. Mary was removed from the care of the Earl of Shrewsbury, who had been her jailer for over a decade, and placed under the care of Sir Amyas Paulet, a much stricter guardian, who reinforced the guard that accompanied Mary when she took exercise outdoors. Because he read all her correspondence, she began smuggling letters out in the only way possible—by entrusting them to the care of her laundresses, the only persons who were allowed to come and go freely from the castle.

Sir Francis Walsingham, who commanded a vast spy network, apprehended a young Catholic priest who was loyal to Mary and persuaded him to become a double agent working against her. This priest informed Mary that he had access to a "secret channel" whereby he could pass her letters along to her friends in Europe without threat of them being read by English security agents. Walsingham's intention was to provide her with the rope she needed to hang herself: by making her believe that she could communicate privately with her co-conspirators, she might be induced to directly incriminate herself in a plot to deprive Elizabeth of her throne, which might finally persuade her to have Mary executed.

Elizabeth's biographer, Alison Weir, suggests that Elizabeth knew about Walsingham's strategy and approved it. She quotes Elizabeth's words to the French ambassador, saying, "You have much secret communication with the Queen of Scotland, but believe me, I know all that goes on in my kingdom. I myself was prisoner in the days of the Queen my sister, and am aware of the artifices that prisoners use to win over servants and obtain secret intelligence."

In 1586, Pope Sixtus V gave his official sanction for the Enterprise of England to proceed under Philip of Spain's direction. Mary Stuart, by this time, had made up her mind to yield her claim on the English throne to Philip; he, in turn, decided to bestow England upon his second child, the Infanta Isabella. For Philip, making war against England was no mere empire-building endeavor—he saw himself as leading a crusade against a heretic queen who had led her people into spiritual darkness. But as a Christian king, he needed an ironclad excuse for making war against England in order to avoid rousing the anger of the other European powers—an excuse that Mary Stuart was shortly to provide.

In the summer of 1586, a Catholic English gentleman named Anthony Babington, who as a boy had been one of Mary Stuart's pages, proposed a plot wherein he, aided by six of his friends, would personally assassinate Elizabeth in her public receiving chambers. Walsingham had Babington under surveillance, and he allowed Babington's letter to reach Mary Stuart, so that she might consent to the plot and thus implicate herself. On July 17th of that year, Mary's reply came:

"The affair being thus prepared, and forces in readiness both within and without the realm, then shall it be time to set the six gentlemen to work; taking order upon the accomplishment of their design, I may be suddenly transported out of this place."

It was nothing less than direct consent for an attempt to murder the Queen of England in her name. Walsingham had what he needed to condemn the Queen of Scots, but he attached a postscript to the letter that would ferret out the identities of the six would-be assassins:

"I would be glad to know the names and qualities of the six gentlemen which are to accomplish the design, for that it may be, I shall be able upon knowledge of the parties to give you some further advice necessary to be followed therein; and even so do I wish to be made acquainted with the names of all such principal persons as also from time to time particularly how you proceed and as soon as you may for the same purpose who be already and how far every one privy hereunto."

It was scarcely a subtle inquiry, but it scarcely mattered: the six gentlemen in question had commissioned a portrait to be painted of them all together, anticipating that they would soon be famous. Walsingham simply had multiple copies of the portrait made, and soon everyone in England knew their faces. They were arrested swiftly, and Babington made a full confession.

The Trial of Mary Stuart

Even at this extremity, Elizabeth was deeply reluctant to involve Mary Stuart in a public trial, and even went so far as to order that all reference to her be struck from Babington's confession and testimony. Her advisors pointed out that the evidence would make very little sense to the court if Mary's name were not mentioned, and Elizabeth capitulated. Babington was convicted and subjected to the full legal penalty for traitors: public hanging, followed by emasculation and disembowelment, then beheading and quartering. Normally, the prisoner was hanged until dead before the rest of the sentence was carried out, but Elizabeth, wishing to make an example of Babington, ordered him cut down after his hanging before he strangled to death, so that he was still alive when the disembowelment began. Public outcry at the cruel manner of his death was so vehement that she allowed the other members of the conspiracy to be executed in the usual manner.

Elizabeth had hoped that the gruesome spectacle of Babington's execution would result in her subjects' feeling that justice had been done, and that there was no need to deal with Mary Stuart in a similar way. That was not to be the case, however. Her councilors pointed out that it would be unfair to punish all the other conspirators and allow Mary to escape trial; furthermore, all of England was frightened and unsettled by how close they had come to invasion and war, and they needed reassurance. Elizabeth refused to allow Mary to be confined in the Tower of London—probably remembering her own terrifying stint there as a prisoner when she was young—but she agreed to have Mary removed to Fotheringay Castle, which was more secure than her present prison. The legality of putting Mary on trial was in question, because Mary was not an English subject, and as an anointed sovereign, was answerable only to God for her actions. However, a special law had been passed in 1583 called the Bond of Accord, which authorized the capture and execution of any person who attempted or succeeded in usurping the throne, or attempted or succeeded in assassinating Elizabeth herself. Under this law, Elizabeth's lawyers reasoned, Mary was eligible for trial and punishment for her actions.

Mary Stuart, unsurprisingly, did not acknowledge that an English court had any jurisdiction to try her, and refused at first to appear in person at the trial or make any response to the charges. But William Cecil urged her to cooperate so that she could clear her name, and Elizabeth, in October of 1586, wrote her the following letter:

"You have in various ways and manners attempted to take my life and to bring my kingdom to destruction by bloodshed. I have never proceeded so harshly against you, but have, on the contrary, protected and maintained you like myself. These treasons will be proved to you and all made manifest. Yet it is my will, that you answer the nobles and peers of the kingdom as if I were myself present. I therefore require, charge, and command that you make answer for I have been well informed of your arrogance.

"Act plainly without reserve, and you will sooner be able to obtain favour of me."

This note convinced Mary to participate in the trial, but she steadfastly denied that she had ever conspired against Elizabeth's life, saying that she had only been attempting to win her freedom. The evidence against her, however, was overwhelming, and the court found her guilty by a nearly unanimous vote. Verdict could only be passed by the Queen and Parliament, however, which meant that Mary Stuart's fate was ultimately in their hands. As Alison Weir puts it,

"Both Lords and Commons loudly demanded Mary's head, and unanimously ratified the commissioners' verdict on 'this daughter of sedition', resolving to petition the Queen that 'a just sentence might be followed by as just an execution'. This petition, which was presented to Elizabeth by a delegation of twenty peers and forty MP's at Richmond on 12 November, plunged her into an agony of indecision."

Elizabeth told the parliamentary delegation that she had written to Mary in secret, informing her that if she would make a full confession, Elizabeth would preserve her life and "cover her shame", but Mary had continued to insist on her innocence. Elizabeth wrote again to warn her that Parliament was demanding her death; Mary's reply is below:

"Now having been informed, on your part, of the sentence passed in the last session of your Parliament, and admonished by Lord Beale to prepare myself for the end of my long and weary pilgrimage, I prayed them to return my thanks to you for such agreeable intelligence, and to ask you to grant some things for the relief of my conscience.

"I will not accuse any person, but sincerely pardon every one, as I desire others, and, above all, God, to pardon me. And since I know that your heart, more than that of any other, ought to be touched by the honour or dishonour of your own blood, and of a Queen, the daughter of a king, I require you, Madam, for the sake of Jesus, that after my enemies have satisfied their black thirst for my innocent blood, you will permit my poor disconsolate servants to remove my corpse, that it may be buried in holy ground, with my ancestors in France, especially the late Queen my mother, since in Scotland the remains of the Kings my predecessors have been outraged, and the churches torn down and profaned.

"As I shall suffer in this country, I shall not be allowed a place near your ancestors, who are also mine, and persons of my religion think much of being interred in consecrated earth. I trust you will not refuse this last request I have preferred to you, and allow, at least, free sepulture to this body when the soul shall be separated from it, which never could obtain, while united, liberty to dwell in peace.

"Dreading the secret tyranny of some of those to whom you have abandoned me, I entreat you to prevent me from being dispatched secretly, without your knowledge, not from fear of the pain, which I am ready to suffer, but on account of the reports they would circulate after my death. It is therefore that I desire my servants to remain witnesses and attestators of my end, my faith in my Saviour, and obedience to His church. This I require of you in the name of Jesus Christ in respect to our consanguinity, for the sake of King Henry VII, your great-grandfather and mine, for the dignity we have both held, and for the sex to which we both belong.

"I beseech the God of mercy and justice to enlighten you with His holy Spirit, and to give me the grace to die in perfect charity, as I endeavour to do, pardoning my death to all those who have either caused or cooperated in it; and this will be my prayer to the end.

"Accuse me not of presumption if, leaving this world and preparing myself for a better, I remind you will one day to give account of your charge, in like manner as those who preceded you in it, and that my blood and the misery of my country will be remembered, where for from the earliest dawn of your comprehension we ought to dispose our minds to make things temporal yield to those of eternity."

Elizabeth spent several months pleading with her Privy Council and Parliament to find some alternative solution to the problem Mary presented. Parliament could scarcely meet for a discussion without the Queen sending word that the session was to be adjourned for a week, or two weeks. She entertained ambassadors who came to speak on Mary's behalf and requested that her oldest friend, Robert Dudley, return from his military campaign in the Netherlands to be with her while Mary's fate was debated. Every person in England except Elizabeth seemed united in the belief that Mary Stuart was deserving of death under the law, but Elizabeth took seriously her cousin's admonition that she would be answerable to God for her treatment of her fellow queen, and suffered many sleepless nights as a result.

At last, on December 2, 1586, the verdict of death was pronounced against Mary to the English public. The result was widespread rejoicing and celebration, but Elizabeth was still uneasy. A warrant was drawn up for Mary's execution; it stalled in draft form for some weeks before Elizabeth would consent to have it copied into its final format. When at last she did sign it, and gave permission for the Great Seal of England to be affixed to it, she wavered at the last moment as to having it sent out. Her Privy Councilors intervened at this point, all ten of them agreeing to have the warrant sent to Paulet at Fotheringay without giving Elizabeth any further opportunity to change her mind, and to share the responsibility equally if she became angry.

The warrant reached Fotheringay on the 7th of February, 1587; Paulet, receiving it, told Mary that she must prepare to die the next morning. She greeted the news cheerfully and spent the rest of the day writing letters. She was beheaded in the Great Hall of Fotheringay Castle at eight o'clock on February 8th, and, having been denied the company of a priest, refused consolation at the hands of the Protestant minister who was standing by to attend to her. "Thou hast cause rather to joy than to mourn, for now shalt thou see Mary Stuart's troubles receive their long-expected end," she said to her ladies, who accompanied her to the block. She then laid herself down and was beheaded with two blows of the executioner's ax before some three hundred witnesses.

When news of the execution reached Elizabeth, she was more than taken by surprise; she was hysterical. Her rage against her councilors was unlike anything they had seen in her twenty-five-year reign, though she had always been prone to outbursts of temper. She ceased to eat or drink until her ladies were reduced to begging her to look after her health, and most of her councilors fled or were temporarily banished from court. Her reaction was partially genuine shock, partially fear of retribution from the Catholic powers in Europe. Even in Scotland, where Mary had been deeply unpopular since Darnley's murder, there was an outcry, although her son, James I, could not chastise Elizabeth too stridently, because he hoped to be named as successor to the English throne when Elizabeth died. Philip of Spain went into mourning for

Mary's death, and Henry III of France condemned it. Within a few months, however, Elizabeth came to see that it had been necessary, and reconciled with her councilors.

Chapter Seven: Gloriana Regina

"I am sure Her Majesty is made of the same stuff of which the ancients believed the heroes to be form, that is, her mind of gold, her body of brass."

Robert Devereaux, Earl of Essex

The Enterprise of England

Mary Stuart had written to Philip of Spain that she intended to bequeath her claim on the throne of England to him. Thus, after her execution, the people of Spain began to consider England as the rightful possession of the Infanta Isabella, his daughter, on whom Philip intended to bestow the throne. However, it was soon realized that Mary had left no formal will stating her intentions; if Philip wanted England for himself, he would have to come and get it. The Spanish Armada, a fleet 130 galleons (war ships) had been in readiness to sail to England since November of 1587, a month after Mary Stuart's execution, and the English navy, which Elizabeth had been building up over the course of nearly a decade, was ordered to stand in readiness for an attack.

Over the course of 1588, Elizabeth ordered all of England to prepare for invasion: new ships were constructed, old ships were repaired, harbors were refurbished. In June of that year, with the invasion imminent, Elizabeth sent the following dispatch to the Marquis of Winchester and the Earl of Sussex, with instructions for increasing the provisions allotted to footmen and horsemen in their territories:

"RIGHT trusty, and right well-beloved cousins, we greet you well... The great preparations of foreign forces, made with a full intention to invade this our Realm and other of our dominions, we gave our directions unto you for the preparing of our Subjects within your Lieutenancies to be in readiness for defense against any attempt, that might be made against us and our Realm. Which our directions we find so well performed, that we cannot but receive great contentment thereby, both in respect of your careful proceedings therein, and also of the great willingness of our people in general, to the accomplishment of that whereunto they were required.

"Showing thereby their great love, and loyalty towards us, which as we accept most thankfully at their hands, acknowledge ourselves infinitely bound to Almighty God, in that it hath pleased him to bless us with so loving and dutiful Subjects: so would we have you make it known unto them on our behalf, forasmuch as we find the same intention not only of invading, but of making a conquest also of this our Realm, now constantly more and more detected, and confirmed as a matter fully resolved on (an Army being already put to the Seas for that purpose which we doubt not but by God's goodness, shall prove frustrate), we have therefore thought meet, to will, and require you forthwith, with as much convenient speed as you may, to call together at some convenient place or places the best sort of gentlemen under your Lieutenancy, and to declare unto them that considering these great preparations and arrogant threatenings now burst out in action upon the Seas, tending to a conquest, wherein every man's particular state is in the highest degree to be touched, in respect of Country, Liberty, Wife, Children, lands, life, and that which is specially to be regarded, for the profession of the true and sincere Religion of Christ and laying before them the infinite and unspeakable miseries, that follow upon any such accident and change (which miseries are evidently seen by the fruits of the hard and cruel government that is held in Countries not far distant, where such change doth happen, whatsoever pretense is otherwise given forth for the cause of Religion) we do look that the most part of them should have, upon this instant extraordinary occasion a larger proportion of furniture, both for horsemen and footmen (but especially horsemen) than hath been certified, thereby to be in there best strength against any attempt whatsoever, and to be employed both about our own person and otherwise, as they shall have knowledge given unto them, the number of which larger proportion as soon as you shall know, we require you to signify to our privy Counsel, hereunto as we doubt not but by your good endeavors, they will be the rather conformable, So also we assure ourselves, that Almighty God will so bless their loyal hearts born towards us their loving Sovereign and their natural Country, that all the attempts of any enemies whatsoever shall be made void and frustrate, to their confusion, your comforts, and to God's high glory."

Elizabeth was anything but a warmongering queen; she had done her utmost to avoid conflict throughout her reign, both within her own borders and with foreign powers, not because she lacked courage but because she knew that wars could be disruptive and ruinous to the lives of her subjects. As such, she was hesitant to hasten the outbreak of the war, but her advisors, particularly Leicester, were insistent that war was coming whether she wished it or not. Sir Franics Drake suggested that he sail to Spain and sabotage the Spanish ships before they set sail, but, according to Weir, Elizabeth believed that "any confrontation...must take place within sight of the shores of England, in order to remind her sailors what they were fighting for." Elizabeth attempted peace negotiations with Spain until the summer of 1688, but by June, war was imminent.

Word reached Elizabeth that the Spanish armada had been sighted off the coast of England on the night of July 22nd. She was resolute in the face of the threat: she had been preparing for this conflict for months, and she knew that the English defenses were as ready as they could be. Philip's goal was to reach the Netherlands, where the Duke of Parma stood in readiness with a Spanish army of 16,000 men, to conduct the land invasion; Elizabeth's goal was to prevent the armada from making harbor. The English fleet, under the joint command of Lord Howard and Sir Francis Drake, numbered 150 ships. On land, Robert Dudley was assembling 4000 troops at Tilbury, an artillery fort in Essex on the north bank of the Thames river and the first waterway defense against the invasion of London. It was to Tilbury that Elizabeth rode on the 8th of August, in order to speak to the troops. Her first desire had been to place herself at the head of her army, "ready to meet Parma when he came", but her advisors suffered a collective apoplexy when she said as much. No English monarch had led an army on a battlefield since Richard III, and the idea of Elizabeth doing so terrified her councilors to the same degree that her courage awed them. Leicester promised that if she came to Tilbury she could do a great deal of good for her soldiers, and he himself would personally ensure her safety. Elizabeth's feeling seems to have been that leading her army in battle was nothing less than her duty as Queen; her councilors' feelings were a cross between outraged chivalry and practical, political concerns about what should happen if Elizabeth were killed in the midst of a war with no successor named. As Leicester put it, her person was "the most dainty and sacred thing we have in this world to care for, [so that] a man must tremble when he thinks of it."

On the first day of fighting, July 28th, the English gained a decisive advantage which the Spanish never recovered from. The armada was bearing down on the coast in a crescent formation, a tight, impenetrable barrier that the smaller, faster, lighter English ships could not hope to break. However, the English took advantage of the close quarters by dispatching "hell-burners", ships loaded with flammable materials such as pitch, to break the line. This maneuver was more successful than they could have dreamed, owing to high, favorable winds that spread the fire and prevented the Spanish from regrouping. The Spanish galleons were forced to scatter, which conferred greater advantage on the more maneuverable English ships. The next day, the Spanish lost eleven ships and two thousand men, while the English lost only fifty men. The day after, the Spanish ships were caught up in a terrible wind that drove them off course; a resulting storm all but destroyed their ships. The English pursued them until they ran out of ammunition, but the storm had done the bulk of the work.

The sea invasion was thus repelled, with the Spanish facing the loss of forty-four of their ships and two-thirds of their men, a disaster on such a scale that many in Spain and England both regarded it as a direct intervention by the hand of God. But there remained the land invasion to face; the Duke of Parma's army of 16,000 were poised to cross the English channel and invade at a moment's notice. Therefore, Elizabeth rode to Tilbury Fort to join Leicester and give encouragement to her troops. Her councilors were just as horrified as they had been previously, but Leicester, perhaps knowing her better than the rest, did not attempt to dissuade her, and instead appointed himself her personal bodyguard. When Elizabeth arrived, she was clad, in Weir's description, "like an angel bright":

"the Queen appeared before her troops in the guise of 'some Amazonian empress' in a white velvet dress with a shining silver cuirass, and preceded by a page carrying her silver helmet on a white cushion and the Earl of Ormonde bearing the sword of state. Leicester had stage-managed the occasion brilliantly, incorporating much pageantry and spectacle. As the tent-flags and pennants fluttered in the breeze, and the drummers and pipers played, the Queen, with tears in her eyes, inspected the immaculate squadrons of foot soldiers, and the well-caparisoned, plumed cavalry...calling out, 'God bless you all!' as many fell to their knees and cried aloud, 'Lord preserve our Queen!'"

The next morning, the soldiers were delighted when Elizabeth paid a second visit to the camp, during which she delivered an address from horseback, wearing an armored breastplate. The speech she delivered was not written down, but it was written down and preserved by one of Elizabeth's war chaplains. The text is below:

"My most loving people, we have been persuaded by some that are careful of our safety, to take heed how we commit our selves to armed multitudes, for fear of treachery; but I assure you

I do not desire to live to distrust my faithful and loving people.

"Let tyrants fear. I have always so behaved myself that, under God, I have placed my chiefest strength and safeguard in the loyal hearts and good-will of my subjects; and therefore I am come amongst you, as you see, at this time, not for my recreation and disport, but being resolved, in the midst and heat of the battle, to live and die amongst you all; to lay down for my God, and for my kingdom, and my people, my honour and my blood, even in the dust.

"I know I have the body but of a weak and feeble woman; but I have the heart and stomach of a king, and of a king of England too, and think foul scorn that Parma or Spain, or any prince of Europe, should dare to invade the borders of my realm; to which rather than any dishonor shall grow by me, I myself will take up arms, I myself will be your general, judge, and rewarder of every one of your virtues in the field.

"I know already, for your forwardness you have deserved rewards and crowns; and we do assure you in the word of a prince, they shall be duly paid you. In the mean time, my Lieutenant General shall be in my stead, than whom never prince commanded a more noble or worthy subject; not doubting that, but by your obedience to my general, by your concord in the camp, and your valor in the field, we shall shortly have a famous victory over those enemies of my God, of my kingdom, and of my people."

The next day, Elizabeth received news that the danger was past. The invasion had been called off, as the Duke of Parma was not willing to risk his troops now that the armada was not available to support them. Philip of Spain was so crushed by his staggering defeat that he and his entire court went into mourning.

The Death of Robert Dudley, Earl of Leicester

Elizabeth's relationship with Robert Dudley was unlike that she shared with any other courtier or subject; friends since they were small children, they had been passionately in love when they were young, and Leicester had spent decades exerting himself to the utmost of his power to convince the Queen to marry him. She had many favorites, and played at romantic games with many handsome male courtiers, but her relationship with Leicester stood apart. They often quarreled, sometimes for months at a time. Leicester's most reliable method for getting back in Elizabeth's good graces after an argument was to take to his rooms and feign sickness; Elizabeth inevitably came to visit him, and forgave him whatever offense he had committed. She had not always been kind to him. When she felt that Leicester was forgetting his place, she was not above humiliating him publicly. But he was never anything but intensely loyal to her, and she relied on him as she could rely on few people.

After Leicester's energetic actions in defense of the realm during the war with Spain, Elizabeth contemplated investing him with the title of Lieutenant Governor of England and Ireland, an unprecedented rank that would make him effectively viceroy of the nation, second in power only to herself. It would have been the next best thing to the crown matrimonial, which he had so coveted in past decades; and it would have befit their relationship, which was more akin to that of a long-married couple than anything else, the affection they bore one another steady and warm where once it had been passionate and uncertain.

Leicester's health had been in decline for a few years prior to the Spanish invasion, and shortly after the armada was repelled his symptoms grew acute. He lived long enough to make a triumphal procession into London, where he was greeted by adoring multitudes, but within a month of the victory he was dead. His final letter to Elizabeth was written on August 26, 1588:

"I most humbly beseech Your Majesty to pardon your old servant to be thus bold in sending to know how my gracious lady doth, and what ease of her late pain she finds, being the chiefest thing in the world I do pray for, for her to have good health and long life. For my own poor case, I continue still your medicine, and it amends much better than any other thing that hath been given me. Thus hoping to find a perfect cure at the bath, with the continuance of my wonted prayer for Your Majesty's most happy preservation, I humbly kiss your foot."

Nine days later, on September 4th, Leicester died, after having been forced to discontinue his journey to the spa baths by a severe fever. He was buried in Warwick next to his son, who had died when he was five years old. Elizabeth was thus bereaved by the loss of her best friend at the very high point of her reign, when the whole country was rejoicing for the victory over Spain. She shut herself away in her rooms for several days, ignoring all affairs of state, to mourn for him privately. Elizabeth seems to have interpreted the loss of Leicester as a kind of divine check to her pride, lest she think too highly of herself after defeating the Spanish. She kept Leicester's final letter in a small chest that sat next to her bed, where it remained until it was discovered after her death. Leicester's final gifts to Elizabeth was a strand of six hundred pearls and an emerald and diamond pendant, which were left to her in his will.

Robert Devereux, Earl of Essex

The decade or so following the victory against the Spanish was marked by a kind of changing of the guard in Elizabeth's court, as the councilors and courtiers who had attended her since she was young began to die off from illness and old age. In several instances, men who had been fixtures in Elizabeth's service were replaced by their own sons. Robert Dudley's step-son, Robert Devereux, the Earl of Essex, was held in great affection by Elizabeth, almost more so than he deserved. He was haughty and short-tempered and often sought to manipulate Elizabeth by protesting his great devotion to her, only to declare himself neglected and ill-used. His chief rival was Robert Cecil, the son of William Cecil, Lord Burghley, who took over Elizabeth's spy service after the death of Sir Francis Walsingham. Sir Walter Raleigh, another of Elizabeth's long-time favorites, fell from grace spectacularly when he impregnated, then secretly married one of her maids of honor, Bess

Throckmorton. Her courtier Sir Christopher Hatton also died during this period; he had been rivals with Leicester for Elizabeth's affections in past decades. The rivalries between the new generation of courtiers, particularly between Essex and Robert Cecil, would lead to bitter factionalism in Elizabeth's court towards the end of her reign. Only Lord Burghley remained alive to serve her, and he was in poor health.

Elizabeth herself remained in excellent health throughout her late fifties, a remarkable accomplishment in an age where the average life span hovered around forty. In the years after the victory against Spain, she was at the peak of her fame and international renown. Every monarch in Europe, Catholic and Protestant, praised her; a mere woman, queen of "half a small island", she had won the greatest military victory in English history since the Battle of Agincourt in 1415, humbling the kings of Spain and France in the process. Compared to when Elizabeth first took the throne in 1559, England had undergone a kind of internal revolution. All the world stood in awe of its queen and its navy. Economic prosperity and domestic accord led to a flourishing in the arts, producing the age of playwrights such as William Shakespeare and Christopher Marlowe. Never had Elizabeth's subjects loved her better.

Ongoing threats to the throne

Philip of Spain considered his war against England as a religious duty, and even after his humiliating defeat in 1588 he refused to give up hope of success. Elizabeth, mindful of the danger, dispatched such English heroes of the armada victory as Francis Drake and Walter Raleigh to attack Philip's ships in foreign ports, with mixed results. The most profitable of these raids was carried out against the port of Cadiz, where Spain was readying a fleet for another invasion. Raleigh was chiefly responsible for the victory in Cadiz, but most of the credit was taken by Essex, whose popularity was beginning to give Elizabeth concern. As one of her favorites, with his title and rank and military credibility, she feared that he would be caught up in plots against her. He was impulsive and arrogant and lacked good judgement, and Elizabeth had reason to suspect that his ambition would lead to no good end.

By 1597, a second Spanish invasion was regarded as a near certainty, in retaliation not only for the armada defeat, but for Cadiz. Essex led two further efforts to attack the Spanish navy in their ports, but was repelled each time by storms. In October, the Spanish armada sailed again, and England once again prepared to repel an invasion; but once again, a violent storm destroyed the Spanish fleet on its journey. Essex was in some disgrace on this occasion, as he had taken the English fleet on an ill fated and unsuccessful raid which would have left England bare of defenses if the armada had come. He, like his step-father, chose to feign a prolonged illness in order to soften the queen's heart to receive him again.

Essex was to fall into even greater error in 1598. Elizabeth had always treated him with a larger degree of indulgence than she usually showed towards courtiers, due not only to her personal fondness for him but because he was the step-son of her oldest friend, young enough to have been her own son. Essex had allowed this preferential treatment to cloud his understanding of her nature. Unlike Leicester, who had watched Elizabeth establish her dominance as a young woman, Essex bordered on treating her as if she were a feeble old woman who could be overruled. Elizabeth had allowed this behavior to a point, but Essex was straying dangerously close to the limits of her tolerance.

Then, in July of 1598, Essex fought with Elizabeth over the appointment of Sir William Knollys as Lord Deputy of Ireland. Essex wanted the appointment to go to one of his political enemies, so that he would be safely out of the way in Ireland. When Elizabeth refused to change her mind, Essex insulted her roundly by turning his back on her, which was forbidden in the royal presence. Elizabeth responded by boxing his ears and telling him to "go to the devil". Essex, infuriated and in the heat of the moment, declared that he would not tolerate such behavior from anyone, even her, and reached for his sword. Other courtiers stepped between him and the queen before he could strike her. After a moment of stunned silence, he fled the court. He would not return until his military services were required in the uprising in Ireland in the autumn of that year. However, Essex came to even greater disaster in Ireland, where his incompetence nearly led to his arrest on treason charges. He would eventually lead an attempted coup against Elizabeth in an effort to force her to name him Lord Protector. He was executed for treason on February of 1601.

Elizabeth's declining years

A German visitor to England during the St. George's Day procession in Greenwich left the following minute observation of Elizabeth as she appeared to him at the age of 65, about four years before her death:

"Next came the Queen, very majestic: her face oblong, fair, but wrinkled; her eyes small, jet-black, and pleasant; her nose a little hooked; her lips narrow and her teeth black; her hair was of an auburn color, but false; upon her head she had a small crown. Her bosom was uncovered, as all the English ladies have it till they marry. Her hands were slender, her fingers rather long, and her stature neither tall nor low; her air was stately, and her manner of speaking mild and obliging... She spoke very graciously, first to one, then to another, in English, French and Italian, for besides being well-skilled in Greek and Latin and these languages, she is mistress of Spanish, Scotch and Dutch. Whoever speaks to her, it is kneeling; now and then she raises some with her hand. Wherever she turned her face, everybody fell down on their knees."

Elizabeth, though an old woman by 16th century standards, was even less willing to discuss the matter of her succession than she had been when she was younger. The attempted coup by Essex only made her more fearful that, if she were to name an heir, she would risk being deposed in his favor before her death. Nonetheless, it was generally understood that the throne would pass to James VI of Scotland, who, though resentful of Elizabeth, had taken care never to offend her in a manner that would lead to direct disinheritance. As Elizabeth grew older, some of her councilors began to correspond with the King of Scots in secret, in the hopes of effecting a smooth transition when Elizabeth died.

The Essex coup, together with the death of Lord Burghley, left Elizabeth depressed and isolated. Once a virtual workaholic, she no longer had the energy or attention to conduct affairs of state as she once had. She feared to show any weakness, yet, in body and spirit, she was weaker than ever. Essex had been enormously popular with the common people, and after his execution Elizabeth's popularity declined; she took this very much to heart, as she had worked ceaselessly throughout her reign to make her people love her.

At the thirteenth Parliament of her reign, Elizabeth was so weak that the weight of her royal robes caused her to sway and nearly faint. But she recovered enough to announce that she was assenting to Parliament's request that she end the practice of royal monopolies, which had wreaked havoc on the economy and driven thousands into workhouses. Parliament was overjoyed by the announcement, and begged permission to send a delegation to the queen's palace to offer their thanks. When she received them, on November 30, 1601, she made what is now the most famous speech of her reign, a speech which one observer declared was worthy to have been inscribed in gold. The "golden speech" went as follows:

"The zeal of which affection tending to ease my People, & knit their hearts unto us, I embrace with a Princely care far above all earthly Treasures. I esteem my People's love, more then which I desire not to merit: And God that gave me here to sit, and placed me over you, knows that I never respected my self, but as your good was conserved in me; yet what dangers, what practices, and what perils I have passed, some, if not all of you know: but none of these things do move me, or ever made me fear, but it is God that hath delivered me.

"And in my governing this Land, I have ever set the last Judgement day before mine eyes, and so to rule, as I shall be Judged and answer before a higher Judge, to whose Judgement Seat I do appeal in that never thought was cherished in my heart that tended not to my People's good.

"And if my Princely bounty have been abused, and my Grants turned to the hurt of my People contrary to my will and meaning, or if any in Authority under me have neglected, or converted what I have committed unto them, I hope God they will not lay their culps to my charge.

"To be a King, and wear a Crown, is a thing more glorious to them that see it, than it is pleasant to them that bear it: for my self, I never was so much enticed with the glorious name of a King, or the royal authority of a Queen, as delighted that god hath made me His Instrument to maintain His Truth and Glory, and to defend this Kingdom from dishonour, damage, tyranny, and oppression; But should I ascribe any of these things unto my self, or my sexly weakness, I were not worthy to live, and of all most unworthy of the mercies I have received at God's hands but to God only and wholly all is given and ascribed.

"The cares and trouble of a Crown I cannot more fitly resemble than to the Drugs of a learned Physician, perfumed with some Aromatical savour, or to bitter Pills gilded over, by which they are made more acceptable or less offensive, which indeed are bitter and unpleasant to take; and for my own part, were it not for Conscience sake to discharge the duty that God hath laid upon me, and to maintain his glory, and keep you in safety; in mine own disposition I should be willing to resign the place I hold to any other, and glad to be freed of the Glory with the Labors, for it is not my desire to live nor to reign longer then my life and reign shall be for your good. And though you have had and may have many mightier and wiser Princes sitting in this Seat, yet you never had nor shall have any that will love you better."

The final lines of the speech reprised a sentiment which appeared in many of Elizabeth's speeches, but never to such good effect. The combination of the speech and the announcement of her decision to break the monopolies caused Elizabeth's waning popularity with her subjects to soar to its former heights. During the final session of that parliament, the Speaker pointed out that, of all the nations of Europe, only England had known perfect stability and tranquility of government during the 42 years of Elizabeth's reign.

Throughout 1602 Elizabeth's public appearances grew fewer in number, though she visited friends and danced and rode horses occasionally. She lived to see the end of the rebellion in Ireland, and to receive a diplomatic envoy from Venice, the first ever sent to Protestant England. When her closest female friend died in November of that year, Elizabeth's spirits and health took a sharp turn for the worse. A few months later, in March of 1603, she developed a fever and cold, along with ulcerated sores in her throat. Always scornful of doctors, she refused to see any. When Robert Cecil begged her to take to her bed and rest, saying that she must do so to ease the minds of her subjects, she retorted: "Little man, the word 'must' is not to be used to princes. If your father had lived, you durst not had said so, but ye know that I must die, and that makes thee so presumptuous." One day shortly afterwards, out of sheer stubbornness and a desire to prove herself, she went into her audience chamber and remained on her feet in the presence of her courtiers for fifteen hours; they could not persuade her to sit down, though she was forced to remain in bed for the next four days.

In late March, Elizabeth took to her bed. She could not speak much, but she listened while her court musicians played soft music, and asked for passages from favorite books to be read to her. At about six in the evening on the 23rd of March, she asked for John Whitgift, Archbishop of Canterbury, to pray for her:

"Her Majesty lay upon her back, with one hand in the bed and the other without. The Archbishop kneeled down beside her and examined her first of her faith; and she so punctually answered all his questions, by lifting up her eyes and holding up her hand, as it was a comfort to all the beholders. Then the good man told her plainly what she was and what she was come to: though she had been long a great Queen here upon Earth, yet shortly she was to yield an account of her stewardship to the King of Kings. After this, he began to pray, and all that were by did answer him."

Elizabeth fell asleep at about ten o'clock that night. She died in her sleep at three in the morning on March 24th, 1603. According to Robert Cecil, he asked her who her successor should be, shortly before she died, and she made a motion mimickng a crown sitting atop a head— a sign that she intended to be succeeded by one who was already a king, namely, James I of Scotland. Whether that was indeed the case, or whether it was a fiction to make the king's arrival in England easier, it is impossible to say. James was notified of his accession to the English throne when a sapphire ring belonging to Elizabeth was dispatched to him by a fast rider, but there was no great public celebration to greet him. England was too deeply in mourning for their queen.

Elizabeth was buried in Westminster Abbey, placed in the same vault as her sister, Mary. Her tomb bears the following inscription: "The mother of this her country, the nurse of religion and learning; for perfect skill of very many languages, for glorious endowments, as well of mind as of body, a prince incomparable."

Other books available by Michael W. Simmons on Kindle, paperback and audio:

Nikola Tesla: Prophet Of The Modern Technological Age

Albert Einstein: Father Of the Modern Scientific Age

Alexander Hamilton: First Architect of the American Government

Thomas Edison: American Inventor

Further Reading

The Life of Elizabeth I, by Alison Weir

Elizabeth's Bedfellow's: An Intimate History of the Queen's Court, by Anna Whitelock

Queen Elizabeth I: Selected Works, by Steven W. May

Letter from Elizabeth Tudor to Katharine Parr, 1544

      http://www.luminarium.org/renlit/elizlet1544.htm

Letter from the Princess Elizabeth to Mary I, 1554

      http://www.luminarium.org/renlit/elizlet4.htm

Speech of Elizabeth I upon her accession

> http://www.theanneboleynfiles.com/the-accession-of-elizabeth-i-17th-november-1558/

Response of Elizabeth I to Parliament's request that she marry, 1559

> http://www.luminarium.org/renlit/response parl1559.htm

Speech of Elizabeth I to Parliament on Religion, 1559

> http://www.luminarium.org/renlit/elizspeec hreligion.htm

Response of Elizabeth I to Parliament's request that she marry, 1566

> http://history.hanover.edu/courses/excerpts/ 165elizabeth.html

Regnans in Excelcis, Pope Pius V, 1570

http://www.papalencyclicals.net/Pius05/p5re
gnans.htm

Elizabeth's speech to the troops at Tilbury

http://www.luminarium.org/renlit/tilbury.ht
m

Elizabeth's "Golden" Speech to Parliament

http://www.luminarium.org/renascence-
editions/eliz1.html

Made in the USA
San Bernardino, CA
11 December 2019